Choices for Efficient

Private Provision

of Infrastructure

in East Asia

Edited by
Harinder Kohli, Ashoka Mody, FLORIDA STATE
and Michael Walton UNIVERSITY LIBRARIES

The World Bank
Washington, D.C.

HC
460.5
.29
C33
1997

The opinions expressed in this report do not necessarily represent the views of the World Bank or its member governments. The World Bank does not guarantee the accuracy of the data included in this publication and accepts no responsibility whatsoever for any consequence of their use. The boundaries, colors, denominations, and other information shown on any map in this volume do not imply on the part of the World Bank Group any judgment on the legal status of any territory or the endorsement or acceptance of such boundaries.

ISBN: 0-8213-4053-0

At the World Bank, Harinder Kohli is senior operations officer in the vice president's office of the East Asia and Pacific Regional Office, Ashoka Mody is principal financial economist in the Project Finance and Guarantees Department, and Michael Walton is director, Poverty Reduction, Poverty Reduction and Economic Management Network.

Contents

Foreword

East Asian economies face important structural challenges that must be addressed if they are to maintain their rapid economic growth, improve living standards, and continue the momentum toward a greater role in the global economy. Two of the challenges broadly confronting the region are meeting the massive demand for infrastructure and adapting the role of the state to the changing economic environment. Unless these challenges are met—and met soon—the region's strong growth cannot be sustained for long.

To promote growth, East Asian economies have traditionally paid greater attention to infrastructure than other developing countries—and their public delivery mechanisms have generally been more efficient. But the continued growth in demand for services, along with changing technology and regulatory approaches, requires a shift from the public to the private sector in infrastructure ownership and service delivery. In infrastructure and elsewhere, East Asian economies are beginning to see a transformation in the role of government and in the regulatory framework for private business. A more hands-off approach is gradually being adopted as increasingly sophisticated economies make strong government intervention both ineffective and unnecessary.

The chapters in this book draw on country experiences—in East Asia and in other regions—to reflect on the options and choices that East Asian policymakers face in infrastructure. They address issues relating to the design of a strategic approach to private involvement, regulatory choices (including the greater play of competition), different methods of contracting private suppliers, management of environmental and resettlement problems when the private sector takes the lead, and new ways of financing private infrastructure.

Earlier versions of the chapters were presented at a high-level conference on private involvement in infrastructure held in Jakarta, Indonesia, in September 1996. Sponsored by the World Bank and the government of Indonesia, this conference brought together East Asian government ministers and senior private sector representatives to identify and discuss major stumbling blocks to broader and more effective private participation in infrastructure.

This book is intended to bring the deliberations of the Jakarta meeting to a wider audience. A second book, *Infrastructure Strategies in East Asia: The Untold Story*, edited by Ashoka Mody, is being simultaneously published by the World Bank's Economic Development Institute. This historical overview of East Asian infrastructure focuses on the traditional public role in planning and delivery. Together, these two books should provide policymakers and the private sector with a more thorough understanding of the often difficult tradeoffs faced when making choices relating to the delivery of infrastructure.

The issues raised in this book form part of the larger agenda of institutional and structural concerns in the region. The development community should continue to explore the issues. East Asia's past successes sometimes lead observers to believe that development has been taken care of. This is by no means the case. Decades of development remain, as well as major challenges. It is my hope that this book will make a valuable contribution to the ongoing debate on the continuing task of development in East Asia and Pacific.

Jean-Michel Severino
Vice President
East Asia and Pacific Region

Making the Next Big Leap: Systemic Reform for Private Infrastructure in East Asia

Harinder Kohli, Ashoka Mody, and Michael Walton

Much is expected of private financing to help meet the infrastructure requirements of the rapidly growing East Asian economies. In the first half of the 1990s private financing did grow briskly. East Asia led the developing world in total international finance for infrastructure, and a sharply growing share of that finance went to private projects (figures 1.1 and 1.2). In 1996 almost $13 billion in international capital flowed to East Asian infrastructure projects, more than $9 billion of it for private activities. Domestic sources provided an estimated $3 billion for private infrastructure.

Despite the growth in private investment, it remains a small share of all infrastructure investment in East Asia, between 12 and 18 percent (although there is much variation in this share across the region). And because much of this investment is backed by implicit or explicit government assurances, the share of private capital at risk is far smaller. Moreover, the growth of private financing slowed in 1996, partly because of the lumpiness typical of infrastructure investments. This book draws on experience in a number of countries—in East Asia and elsewhere—to analyze the impediments to and prospects for private financing of infrastructure.

The challenges in achieving substantial private risk-taking are many. Most East Asian economies have adopted an incremental approach to private participation in infrastructure. They have sought private investment mainly for specific projects, ring-fenced to insulate them from the existing structure of delivery. The result has been variable flows of investment, typically backed by substantial government support. Recognizing the limits to private involvement under the incremental approach, some countries are undertaking broader policy and institutional reforms aimed at creating an environment more conducive to private participation, but these efforts are still at an early stage. Designing such reforms, improving methods of contracting with private parties, building regulatory capacity, and developing domestic capital markets remain on the policy agenda in all the region's economies.

The chapters in this book illustrate the policy concerns and choices in moving toward efficient private involvement in infrastructure. Choices arise in the strategy and organization of reform—with regard to sector, the extent of private participation, the speed of reform, and the planning and coordinating roles of the government. Choices must also be made in the methods for contracting and regulation, the management of environmental and resettlement issues, and the development of financing mechanisms to increase access to long-term funds. The chapters draw on experience in a range of countries—Australia, Chile, and India as well as economies in East Asia—to show what choices are available and what strategies governments have followed. Experiences from outside East Asia illustrate the payoffs of a more integrated and concerted move toward private provision of infrastructure.

This overview chapter describes the recent trends in international financing of infrastructure projects in East Asia, discusses the key policy and institutional impediments to greater private participation, and assesses the role of

**Figure 1.1 East Asia leads the developing world
in international finance for infrastructure . . .**

*Infrastructure financing raised by developing countries,
1986–96 (US$ billions)*

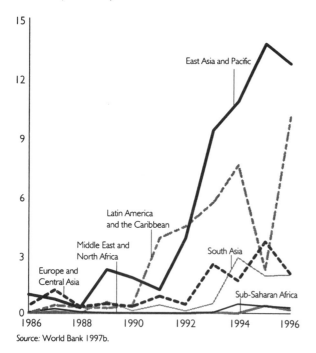

Source: World Bank 1997b.

**Figure 1.2 . . . and devotes a growing share of it
to private projects**

*International infrastructure financing raised in East Asia, by type
of borrower, 1986–96 (US$ billions)*

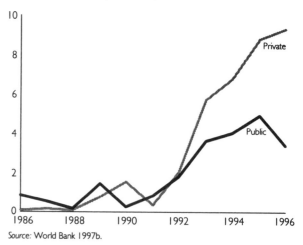

Source: World Bank 1997b.

domestic capital markets and finance. It then outlines a national and regional strategy for stimulating private investment in infrastructure.

Trends in international financing for infrastructure

East Asia's appetite for infrastructure finance is evident in the numbers.[1] In 1996 East Asian economies received $12.7 billion for infrastructure through equity, loan syndications, and bond issues, absorbing just under half of the $27.4 billion in infrastructure finance received by all developing countries.[2] Three-quarters of the international flows to East Asia—$9.3 billion—went to private projects. In the rest of the developing world too, the private sector's share in international capital flows for infrastructure increased steadily over the 1990s, from about a third in 1991 to three-quarters in 1996 ($11 billion). Indeed, in 1996 the flows to public projects fell sharply, from about $5 billion to just over $3 billion.

A distinguishing feature of private capital flows to East Asia is the large share going to new projects rather than to finance the transfer of

assets in privatizations. Between 1984 and 1996 the number of privatization transactions in Latin America was about the same as the number of new investment transactions; in East Asia, by contrast, there were only a third as many privatization transactions as new investment transactions (World Bank, Private Sector Development Department, Private Infrastructure Project Database). Privatization drew 20 percent of the financial flows for infrastructure into East Asia in 1993, 35 percent in 1994, and less than 10 percent ($800 million of $8.7 billion) in 1995 (World Bank, International Economics Department, Privatization Database).

Recipients of the investment

No single country in East Asia has dominated in international finance for private infrastructure projects. In 1995 and 1996 Indonesia was the largest recipient, however, receiving almost $4 billion in each of these years—40 percent of all flows to private infrastructure projects in the region (table 1.1). Private capital for infrastructure accounted for about a third of all private flows into Indonesia in 1995 and a fourth in 1996. Before 1995, however, the largest annual capital inflow for private infrastructure into Indonesia was $339 million, in 1992. The huge jump in 1995 and 1996 reflects primarily the financing of a few large independent power projects whose negotiations, under way for many years, had finally

Table 1.1 International finance for private infrastructure in selected East Asian economies, 1986–96

(US$ millions)

Country	1986	1987	1988	1989	1990	1991	1992	1993	1994	1995	1996
China	0	0	0	0	0	0	761	145	212	185	904
Indonesia	0	0	34	0	0	0	339	0	161	3,690	3,809
Korea, Rep. of	75	160	12	0	957	285	330	105	374	772	1,164
Lao PDR	0	0	0	0	0	0	0	0	0	0	20
Macao	0	0	0	0	0	0	0	0	246	0	0
Malaysia	10	0	42	767	266	31	240	1,135	3,714	1,074	703
Philippines	0	0	0	0	23	39	336	707	1,044	2,135	1,072
Thailand	0	0	0	0	291	0	20	3,619	1,015	936	1,622
Vietnam	0	0	0	0	0	0	0	0	0	5	12
Total	85	160	88	767	1,537	355	2,026	5,711	6,766	8,797	9,306

Source: Euromoney; Loanware; Bondware; World Bank staff estimates.

been completed. In addition, the partial privatization of the telecommunications authority drew in equity flows, and the award of telecommunications concessions at about the same time created demand for financing to meet the investment obligations under the contracts.

Nor does any other economy in East Asia show a clear, strong trend (figure 1.3). Perhaps the most consistent growth has been in the Philippines, however. From virtually none in 1991, private investment in infrastructure in the Philippines grew rapidly until 1995, when international capital flows for infrastructure were just over $2 billion. But in 1996 the flows fell to $1 billion. The fast growth was due to the private power program for installation of more than 3,000 megawatts of power. Now that the program's objectives have been substantially met, the investments in private power generation are tapering off. But demand for private infrastructure finance in the Philippines has been sustained by deregulation in telecommunications, allowing entry by new providers.

Other countries show a choppy pattern. In Malaysia international flows rose from a small amount in 1991 to $3.7 billion in 1994, then declined in 1995 and 1996. Thailand had a peak inflow of $3.6 billion in 1993 but has had much smaller flows since then. But both countries, particularly Malaysia, have had significant domestic financing.

China may be the dominant user of international capital flows for infrastructure in the coming years. Inflows into China jumped to $900 million in 1996, with increasing activity in power and transport. Although private investment in infrastructure remains well below projections, both the government and the private

sector have taken actions likely to boost it. The government has prepared a model for build-operate-transfer projects and applied it to the Laiban power project. The private sector has recently raised funds by securitizing existing projects and then issuing shares on the Hong Kong (China) and Shenzhen stock exchanges. This financing strategy marks a shift from pure project finance—where financing is based only on project cash flows and revenues—to a corporate finance, or pooled, structure, which generally gives greater comfort to lenders.

Sectoral shifts

The capital flows for private infrastructure in East Asia have clearly been driven by independent power generation and telecommunications. While in Latin America telecommunications has taken a

Figure 1.3 No East Asian country shows a clear trend in international financing for private infrastructure

International financial flows to private infrastructure as a percentage of GDP, 1986–96

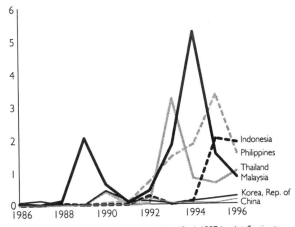

Source: Euromoney; Loanware; Bondware; World Bank 1997d and staff estimates.

Figure 1.4 Loans have been the main source of international finance for private infrastructure in East Asia

Financing for private infrastructure projects, by source, 1986–96 (US$ billions)

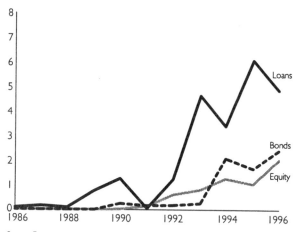

Source: Euromoney; Loanware; Bondware; World Bank staff estimates.

decisive lead, in East Asia neither sector has dominated. Power took the lead in 1992, but was overtaken by telecommunications after a substantial investment in Thailand in 1993, and since then the two sectors have traded the lead a few times.

Despite some privatization of telecommunications in East Asia, a substantial share of the flows into the sector has come through build-operate-transfer schemes (in Indonesia and Thailand) that give private operators responsibilities in a geographic area for a fixed period. The investment commitments for these projects require "lumpy" financing. By contrast, much of the flow into Latin America has come through privatization of state-owned assets, followed by steady growth in new investments. Both regions have received relatively low levels of financing for transportation projects in recent years—not surprising given the problems faced by many such projects. But international finance statistics underestimate transportation investment in East Asia, since domestic capital markets, especially in Malaysia and Thailand, have been active in financing transport activities.

The changing instruments

The mix of financing instruments in East Asia differs from that in Latin America, reflecting the differences in the sectoral pattern of demand for financing. Following the privatization of assets, Latin American infrastructure enterprises have turned to bond and equity markets for most of their international financing. In East Asia there has been a significant rise in international bond and equity finance, but syndicated loans have been the main source of finance, accounting for more than half in 1996 and an even larger share in 1995 (figure 1.4). This is explained largely by private power projects, which have relied mostly on syndicated loans, with debt-to-equity ratios in the range of 75 to 25. In East Asia telecommunications financing, like financing for private power, has followed the limited recourse model (in which repayments are based largely on the project's ability to refinance the debt). The telecommunications sector has relied more on bond and equity issues than has the power sector, but syndicated loans have also been important.

Policies and institutions for private infrastructure

The review of international finance for private infrastructure in East Asia shows that the flows are significant relative both to public flows and to flows to other regions.[3] But investment has been low relative to expectations. There has been much activity in signing memoranda of understanding and even in signing actual contracts: in mid-1996 some $120 billion worth of projects were reported as past the contract award stage. But the recent history of long development periods and high attrition rates for projects suggests that many now under discussion could unravel before financial closure. World Bank estimates of investment requirements in infrastructure for the next decade are $1.2–$1.5 trillion (World Bank 1995b). With international finance for private projects totaling some $9 billion a year in 1995 and 1996 and domestic finance playing a modest role in most countries, a fillip is clearly needed to ensure the infrastructure expansion critical to sustaining East Asia's development in the next century (box 1.1).

Is the slow progress in private investment in infrastructure a sign of intrinsic problems with private involvement? Is there, for example, a limit on the availability of long-term financing? Participants at the Jakarta conference tended to suggest not. The key constraints lie in the framework for private provision of infrastructure. It is the resulting lack of bankable, low-risk projects, not the lack of finance, that is at the heart of the present predicament. But this is not to deny the importance of increasing long-term finance—and of developing weak domestic capital markets in most East Asian economies.

What is the target?

Although the share of private investment in East Asian infrastructure is between 12 and 18 percent, this overall figure is pulled down by the low private share in China. The high level of private involvement in some East Asian economies suggests that the prospects for private participation are much greater than current levels in most of the region.

Hong Kong (China) has traditionally had considerable private involvement in all sectors except water (Kwong 1997). Much private provision has also occurred in Malaysia, where power, transport, water, and telecommunications have all had some infusion of private capital (Naidu and Lee 1997). It is difficult to determine the extent of private investment in Malaysia because the government has continued to have a significant financial commitment even in "private" projects through equity in privatized enterprises and through grants of land rights, direct subsidies, and concessional loans. But it is likely that the private share is more than half.

Private involvement is also high in the Philippines, where World Bank estimates suggest that about 40 percent of new investment in infrastructure has been financed through private projects (Mikesell 1997). Much of the investment in private power projects has benefited from government backing of the payment obligations of the National Power Corporation (box 1.2). The recent spurt of private investment in Indonesia probably places it at the same level as the Philippines. The Indonesian government has refused to provide guarantees, but its "comfort letters" have been viewed by the market as assurances that obligations will be honored.

Elsewhere in East Asia private investment in infrastructure has been limited. But most economies are gearing up for greater private

Box 1.1 Why expanding infrastructure services in East Asia is critical to its future

A continued push to develop infrastructure services in East Asia is crucial to its development as it enters the 21st century. Why?

- *Growth.* Demand for modern infrastructure grows at least as fast as the overall economy—and for many sectors significantly faster. Failure to meet this demand could undercut the potential rapid growth. If investment is not boosted in China's increasingly congested transport system, for example, the economy's growth will be choked off. The government of the Republic of Korea estimates that infrastructure shortages resulted in a gross domestic product some 16 percent short of its potential in the mid-1990s.
- *Competitiveness.* Good power, transport, and telecommunications services are necessary in rich and poor economies alike to sustain growth and competitiveness in an increasingly integrated world. In Indonesia industrial firms that use captive power pay more than twice the price of power from the grid.
- *Quality of life.* Poor infrastructure services mean a poor quality of life despite rapidly rising incomes—especially in urban areas. In many countries households' access to services remains far lower than would be predicted on the basis of income levels. Poor households that have to buy water from vendors pay some sixty times the price of piped water in Bandung and almost twenty times the price in Manila and Ho Chi Minh City. Congestion in cities from Bangkok to Shanghai adds hours to people's daily commute, in air quality conditions way below World Health Organization standards.

Source: World Bank 1994 and 1995b.

participation. China has made progress in the power generation sector with the introduction of model contracts for the Laiban power project. It has recently had success too with pooling existing power projects to attract fixed income investors, using the proceeds for new project development. Pooling structures are also being used for toll road projects (see the section below on financing mechanisms). The Republic of Korea has historically had little private involvement in infrastructure. But it recently raised its target for private financing of infrastructure requirements, aiming for a 40 percent share by 2001–02, up from the original target of 10 percent.

Box 1.2 Managing guarantees in the Philippines

In July 1987 the Philippine government launched a program to attract private investment for power generation (World Bank 1994, p. 67). The government provided full faith and credit guarantees to back the obligations of the National Power Corporation under long-term power purchase agreements with private suppliers. These guarantees covered the entire risk of the corporation's payments: failure to pay for any reason would trigger the guarantee. With much experience in private power generation and thus a track record of honoring payment obligations, the government is in a position to scale back on the guarantees it provides. In 1995 it adopted a policy aimed at doing so, with four objectives:

- To unbundle the risks so as to be able to sharply demarcate covered risks.
- To reduce coverage to 75–80 percent of payment obligations.
- To introduce the concept of guarantee "fall-away" (for example, the guarantee of foreign exchange coverage falls away when the Philippine government achieves an investment-grade credit rating and retains that rating for two years).
- To create administrative mechanisms for more careful review, pricing, and budgeting of guarantees, including possibly retaining reserves against guarantee claims.

The principles of risk unbundling, reduced coverage, and guarantee fall-away have already been adopted in some recent guarantees. Now the Philippine government is investigating options for a present value budgeting system that would reduce the budgetary incentives to provide guarantees (such incentives arise because issuing a guarantee requires no cash, so that no financial charge is made against the department or agency authoring the guarantee).

Source: Philippines 1995.

But experience outside East Asia (and in Malaysia and Hong Kong, China) shows that much higher shares of private infrastructure investment are possible. The most striking shifts toward private investment have occurred in Argentina and Hungary, where at least 70 percent of infrastructure investment is private. In Chile the private sector's share in infrastructure investment is about half (Mikesell 1997).

The Chilean experience offers a contrast to the East Asian strategy (see chapter 4). In Chile the energy and telecommunications sectors are now almost fully private, there is growing private involvement in transport, and a major privatization of water is planned. What has Chile's strategy been? Rather than experiment with ways to attract investment to specific projects in power and telecommunications, it has focused on creating market structures and regulatory institutions conducive to private entry. The result: privatized sectors are seeing rapid investment, face no financing constraints, and receive no explicit or implicit public sector support. Chile has grown 7 percent a year for a decade and, like most East Asian economies, faces rapidly expanding demand for infrastructure services. Of a total projected infrastructure investment of $18 billion over the next six years, some $13 billion—72 percent—is expected to come from the private sector.

In East Asia the scale of private sector involvement in infrastructure will depend on societal preferences and on institutional and policy conditions. Major infrastructure segments, such as feeder roads, will probably continue to be publicly financed, and in most of the region's economies well over half of spending in the next decade will be public. Traditional concerns about improving the efficiency of public sector investment programs and infrastructure operation and maintenance will continue to be important.

Setting up the policy and institutional framework

A recurrent theme in this volume is the importance of a clear policy and institutional framework for private involvement to simultaneously tackle four related objectives:

- Reducing the price distortions and risk factors that are central causes of the weak pipeline of bankable projects.
- Ensuring that projects are approved efficiently, fairly, and in a timely fashion.
- Ensuring that private providers deliver high-quality services efficiently and at reasonable cost.
- Dealing with important societal concerns about the environment, resettlement, and the provision of basic services to the poor.

Not all elements of the framework need be in place before private entry begins. Indeed, many conference participants emphasized that there is no magic formula, and most countries have been proceeding in an evolutionary, learning-by-doing fashion. But an evolutionary policy does

Box 1.3 Risks along the project cycle

Project development, when risks are greatest, is financed almost entirely with equity funds. A drawn-out contract award process and a lack of transparency can greatly increase project preparation costs, so high returns are expected from this exploratory work.

During the construction period project sponsors typically seek 70 percent debt financing. Since capital markets tend to be cautious about financing construction, banks are called on to play a prominent role, and because of the risks demand relatively large spreads. Since commercial bank resources are limited—and there are few banks experienced in international project finance—it is important to recycle bank resources into new projects by refinancing projects through capital markets once they are operational. In principle, governments do not bear construction risk in most projects, but as ultimate guarantors in many projects they do bear residual risk.

Once projects are up and running, cash flows are subject to market and regulatory risks. The solution is to reduce the regulatory risks before operation by establishing sound sectoral frameworks, including for the environment and for resettlement.

not come without costs. From the perspective of potential private investors, evolution is policy instability and a lack of strategic commitment, and it can substantially raise their perceived risks and required returns. Addressing these concerns sometimes will mean striking a balance between efficiency and the need to maintain commitments to the private sector when the rules of the game change because of deeper sectoral reforms. Authorities in Victoria, Australia, struck such a balance by grandfathering a guarantee to a major power project.

In laying out the elements of a sustainable policy framework, conference participants emphasized two aspects of infrastructure delivery. First, there are different phases in an infrastructure project and each has distinct risks (box 1.3). Private sector representatives expressed great concern about risks in the development phase—in the contracting process, the granting of permits, and the management of environmental and resettlement issues. There was also concern about risks during the operational phase, such as changes in contractual agreements (including early termination), inability to obtain payment for services rendered, and inability to convert domestic into foreign currency. Projects in water

and transport may also face direct market risk. Recognizing these risks is a first step in designing government policies and institutions that minimize them.

Second, there are important differences between infrastructure activities that are potentially competitive and those that are intrinsically monopolistic (box 1.4). Natural monopolies require special measures to prevent the granting of favors to potential monopolists, limit the abuse of monopoly power, encourage efficient service provision, and ensure the maintenance of asset quality. Much of the initial private sector activity in East Asia has been in telecommunications and power generation, both potentially competitive activities.

The following sections outline how the four objectives—reducing price distortions and risk factors, ensuring timely and fair project approval, ensuring low-cost, high-quality services, and addressing societal concerns—can be achieved, in monopolistic and potentially competitive activities and in all project phases.

Managing the transition in potentially competitive activities

The countries that have gone furthest in private involvement in infrastructure have all used competition in power and telecommunications. Of the countries represented at the Jakarta workshop, Australia, Chile, and Malaysia have multiple, competing operators in telecommunications. This approach is based on the view that, since there are several technical options for supplying services (radio, satellite, cable networks, traditional wire lines), there is little reason to restrict new entry into telecommunications networks. In power generation Chile and the Australian state of Victoria have competitive structures.

Competition in East Asia is extremely limited, even in telecommunications. Indonesia and Thailand have awarded private telecommunications providers concessions to serve specific geographical areas, but have also granted them monopoly rights in those areas. Awarding concessions to several providers creates the potential for "yardstick" competition, in which suppliers are rewarded on the basis of comparisons with suppliers in other jurisdictions, but

Box 1.4 Policy issues in competitive and monopolistic infrastructure sectors

Technological change has made power generation and long-distance telecommunications potentially competitive and will soon do the same for electricity distribution and local calls. Many other activities are at least in part natural monopolies, especially network industries, such as electricity transmission, gas and water supply, and road and rail transport.

Different policy issues arise in monopolistic and competitive activities. In natural monopoly sectors consumers can often turn to higher-cost alternatives, such as water vendors, alternative energy sources, or competing transport modes. But substantial market power and special pricing problems remain as policy issues. Competition is a desirable goal, but achieving and enforcing it can be a demanding task for policymakers. Relapses into monopoly characteristics are common.

Policy objectives in competitive and monopolistic infrastructure sectors

	Development phase	Service delivery phase
Potentially competitive sectors (electricity generation, long-distance telecommunications)	• Designing market structures for the public to private transition. • Establishing rules for environmental and resettlement issues. • Reducing the public sector's direct role in contracting.	• Implementing general competition policy, including network interconnection arrangements. • Providing explicit subsidies for basic services for the poor.
Natural monopolies (electricity transmission and distribution, toll roads, ports, water supply)	• Efficiently managing the contracting process, using "competition for the market." • Managing environmental and resettlement issues.	• Regulating the sector to ensure fair pricing, low-cost service delivery, high-quality service, and adequate future investment. • Providing explicit subsidies for basic services for the poor.

Source: World Bank 1994; Smith and Klein 1994.

this type of competition is necessarily weaker than direct competition.

In power generation in East Asia private entry has been through long-term, take-or-pay power purchase agreements between private suppliers and government-owned power companies. Under a take-or-pay contract the power company makes a commitment to pay the private operator a capacity fee, which typically covers at least debt and operating costs, whether or not it actually uses the power. Thus, even where there are multiple private generators, they do not compete directly. Investments under such contracts typically occur through build-operate-transfer (BOT) arrangements and are primarily a device to help governments finance new capacity by deferring payments.

The experiences of both Chile and Victoria, Australia, in introducing competition in power supply illustrate gains in both efficiency and investment. Victoria attracted surprisingly high bids on assets sold even without offering a commitment through a take-or-pay contract (box 1.5). While the models for introducing competition differ from one country to another, they share the goal of stimulating competition for

"spot" supply—the daily supply to the transmission grid. In spot markets only the plants able to win the right to supply the daily grid requirements on the basis of their low costs are paid. There is an incipient movement in the Philippines to create competition in power supply along these lines.

Other countries in East Asia are also considering sectoral reforms in power. Reform is high on the agenda in China, for example. Countries where private entry is at an early stage can skip the stage based on BOTs and power purchase guarantees. But there are important preconditions for successful competition. The utility buying power must be creditworthy, or new entry is unlikely to occur. Price reforms are necessary to ensure the sector's viability. Reforms of the power utility may also be needed, often including privatization. And competition requires a regulatory infrastructure, including "power pools" and mechanisms to ensure fair dispatch (and thus the choice of generating plants with the lowest marginal cost of supply).

Competition eases the task of regulation, since it fosters efficiency and fair pricing. But merely permitting new entry is not always

Box 1.5 Beyond power purchase agreements—managing the transition to competition in power generation

In the Philippines a framework for competitive electricity supply is beginning to emerge and will probably be put in place in the next three to five years. The country will then have to decide how to handle existing power purchase agreements. For guidance, it can look to the Australian state of Victoria, which has already made the transition to competition.

The first major private entry in Victoria's power generation sector was through the sale of the half-finished, 1,000-megawatt Loy Yang B plant. Negotiations were long, costly, and complex but eventually ended in a deal involving a thirty-three-year take-or-pay power purchase agreement and the state electricity utility taking all the construction risk. When Victoria later introduced full competition in generation and complementary reforms in transmission and distribution, it chose to grandfather the power purchase agreement with Loy Yang B in order to avoid destabilizing the business environment—despite potential efficiency losses.

The priority given to a stable business environment, combined with deep sectoral reforms, has led to strong private interest—without the government having to offer guarantees. One measure of private interest is the purchase of the thirty-year-old Hazelwood power plant for three times its book value, with no power purchase agreement. This sale, along with sales of distribution companies, has helped transform the state's finances.

Source: Russell in this volume.

Box 1.6 Leaving the contracting choice to the market—the gas pipeline in Chile

A pipeline to transport natural gas over the Andes from Argentina is an important option for energy supply in Chile. Once constructed, such a pipeline would be a natural monopoly. Negotiations to construct a pipeline started between the government and potential developers, who emphasized the need for government guarantees to make the project viable. But the government, judging that it had little basis on which to negotiate, left the developers to negotiate directly with the potential users. Of the two consortia that competed for the right to serve customers, one eventually struck a deal with a group of consumers at a price far lower than that originally proposed to the government—with no government guarantee of the purchase contracts.

Source: Jadresic in this volume.

enough to make market structures competitive. Market structures created at the time of restructuring or privatization can have long-lasting influences. Chile allowed a vertically integrated power company, creating a potential for the company, as owner of the grid, to give preference to the generating plants it owned. By contrast, Victoria, Australia, moved to five generating companies and an independently owned grid when it deregulated. Even after the principle of competition is established, the regulator or competition authority needs to keep an eye out for anticompetitive tendencies.

Ensuring competition for the market and timely and efficient contracting

Many infrastructure projects are not in competitive activities, either because they are natural monopolies or, as in much of the power and telecommunications investment in East Asia, because service provision has not yet been deregulated. Investment in noncompetitive activities generally implies direct government management of the choice of project and the award of contract, an approach that raises different concerns for the public and private sectors. Government representatives at the conference particularly emphasized the need to ensure fair deals for society and avoid the excessive profits (and political fallout) associated with highly favorable contracts. Private sector representatives expressed concern about lack of clarity in the rules of contracting and the cost of the process, which is financed entirely with equity and must therefore yield a high return.

Where direct competition in supply is limited, another potential source of discipline is competition "for the market," or for the right to supply. Such competition requires governments to identify projects, invite competitive bids, evaluate the bids, and award contracts. To exploit the potential of such competition, governments need to establish the basic rules and legal framework for eligible projects, identify qualified suppliers, and conduct individual transactions that result in prices that are fair and beneficial to consumers and are perceived as such. Where private involvement is mature and consumers are well informed, the government can withdraw from the contracting process—as the Chilean government did in natural gas supply (box 1.6).

East Asia already has some of the basic legal structure in place for private sector entry, but a large agenda of legal reform lies ahead. In such countries as Cambodia, Mongolia, and Vietnam, where no private projects have been implemented, the rules for BOT projects are still in the early stages of development. In China several private projects are in operation, but the BOT policy continues to evolve. Laws permitting water and road concessions are needed in most countries, as are extensive legal changes to allow privatization of state assets. Several conference participants stressed the need for a legal structure that would increase confidence in the contracting process among potential suppliers and eventual consumers and thus lower the costs of completing transactions.

The economic and social benefits of a project also depend to a great extent on how the contract is procured. While the choice between competitive and noncompetitive procurement is often—and quite rightly—emphasized, other features of the transaction can also substantially influence the outcome. Early contracts in a country or sector are often negotiated directly with selected parties rather than offered for competitive bid. The Philippines, for example, used direct negotiations in its initiative to attract private investors to the power sector during the emergency period of blackouts. But in recent transactions it has relied on competitive sourcing; several bidders have typically responded, resulting in substantial competition and a steady lowering of the purchase price for power. Another successful example of competitive procurement has been in Thailand, where bidders were invited concurrently to bid on projects to provide up to 4,000 megawatts of power. Competition was extensive, and commitments to supply were obtained at the low end of the international range. Competitive bidding was also effectively used in Indonesia for telecommunications contracts.

The disadvantages of noncompetitive bidding processes are well known: high prices and indifference to consumer needs often result. But despite the obvious benefits of competitive bids, many projects are still procured through direct solicitation or in response to private sector proposals. For example, in Malaysia, which has the largest portfolio of private projects in East Asia, virtually all projects have been directly procured. Proponents of noncompetitive bids cite several benefits. The procurement process takes less time. Overall preparation costs are lower, since the costs that would have been incurred by unsuccessful bidders are eliminated. And unlike in a competitive situation, in which all bidders must respond to a common basic request for proposals, the private sponsor has the opportunity to show innovation in project design.

Examples presented at the conference showed that the gap between competitive and noncompetitive contracting can be narrowed by overlaying on one the positive features of the other. For example, a government could subject a sole-source bid to an open and competitive price challenge before the award, while giving the initial bidder some preference based on its early design and development costs. The costs of project preparation could be subsidized to attract a larger number of bidders, a practice used in the United Kingdom's private sector initiative and likely to be adopted in the Philippines. In South Australia authorities conducted a negotiation process with competing bidders that was akin to that for sole-sourced contracts (box 1.7). Whatever the approach to contracting, preparatory work by the government is critical to success.

Just as competitive and noncompetitive contracting can share the presumed benefits of the other, they can also share each other's presumed ills. Transparency of process, with a heavy emphasis on information disclosure, is critical, regardless of whether a contract is procured competitively. While a suspicion of political patronage is almost inevitable in directly negotiated deals, a competitive process can also be tainted—or at least perceived to be so. There should be no presumption that competitive bidding will be fairly and transparently conducted. Witness the heavy controversy surrounding the award of a water treatment contract in Thailand and a set of telecommunications contracts in India. Lack of clarity on the criteria used in choosing the winning bidder and a perception that the rules of the game have changed midway through the bidding process are typical sources of controversy.

Three messages emerge from the experience in contracting for infrastructure provision.

Competition can bring major gains in price. Whether the contracting is competitive or not, transparency is highly desirable on both efficiency and political grounds. And some of the positive features of direct negotiations can be incorporated into competitive bidding.

Using regulation to promote efficiency

However carefully contract award is conducted, it generally must be followed by continual project oversight to ensure that contract terms are met and that unexpected effects are not interfering with societal concerns. Such ongoing oversight is referred to as regulation. As with contract award, the process—and thus the transparency and accountability—of regulation is at least as important as its technical features.

East Asia has limited experience with modern regulatory practices, but conference participants agreed that the region's governments need to adopt such practices. These practices are increasingly based on exploiting the incentives of service providers to behave in a socially desirable manner. This "incentive regulation" minimizes the information required by the regulator to do its job. By contrast, rate-of-return regulation, now rarely used, imposes high information requirements. In this type of regulation prices are set so as to ensure that the provider receives a specified rate of return, a system that creates a perverse incentive for the provider to increase capital costs while giving the regulator the difficult task of determining the appropriate level of investment. Another, increasingly popular method of price regulation limits prices (or their rate of growth) rather than rates of return. Under this "price cap" system providers have an incentive to minimize costs.

A price cap system does require benchmark estimates of rates of return at the time the cap, or limit, is established. But once set, price caps need be adjusted only every five to seven years, limiting the information required for effective regulation. Price caps are being used in power generation contracts throughout East Asia, although an important contract for a national sewerage system in Malaysia is being regulated on a rate-of-return basis.

Box 1.7 Managing competition in contracting—South Australia's experience in water supply

The award of a water supply contract in South Australia shows how a competitive bid can incorporate some of the presumed benefits of directly negotiated contracts.

- Prospective bidders were provided detailed technical and financial information based on past operation by the public sector, but they also were invited and expected to undertake their own due diligence, including assessing demand.
- The authorities announced detailed criteria for choosing the winning consortium and for conducting any renegotiations. Renegotiation can occur even in competitive situations, and prespecifying the criteria to be used ensures greater transparency.
- After receiving proposals from four prequalified bidders, the authorities entered into a relatively novel—and potentially delicate—set of parallel negotiations with the bidders. They took elaborate precautions to prevent the abuse of confidential information, and they validated the assumptions underlying each bidder's proposal, limiting the possibility of postcontractual renegotiations.
- The bidding process was completed in eighteen months under the supervision of highly experienced professionals, including international consultants.

Source: South Australia, Ministry for Industry, Manufacturing, Small Business, and Regional Development; South Australia Water Corporation.

Regardless of the method of regulation, measures are required to ensure the accountability and independence of regulators so that their decisions will carry authority. If the relationship between the regulator, the legislature, and the executive is blurred, as it typically is, it will need to be clarified. One view holds that the regulator should be accountable to the legislature, with regulatory commissions staffed by members with overlapping terms so that an entire commission cannot be summarily dismissed.

Dealing with broader societal concerns

Discussions in Jakarta emphasized the importance of dealing with societal concerns explicitly and early, often with both public and private involvement. Doing so allows risks and opportunities to be addressed efficiently. For example, dealing with environmental and resettlement concerns during project development opens opportunities for innovative, "win-win" solutions. Similarly, to ensure that the goals of expanded service coverage and affordable services for the poor are met, they need to be clearly stated up front and reflected in the regulatory framework and pricing structures.

Resettlement is frequently an important concern in infrastructure projects, particularly in transportation and hydroelectric projects, and it can become a major source of project risk if not handled carefully. Governments in East Asia are devising policies and procedures for resettling those displaced by infrastructure projects. Projects involving international lending agencies face increased pressure for effective design and implementation of resettlement plans. But even in projects with purely private investment, the risk of political opposition requires active government involvement to ensure that the concerns of those affected are fairly and equitably addressed through consultation, choice of suitable relocation sites, and adequate support (including compensation) to restore long-term incomes (box 1.8).

Dealing with environmental concerns similarly requires careful, thorough planning. Most project sponsors tend to view environmental concerns as a source of increased project cost and risk, both during project development and later on, as unexpected liabilities arise due to changes in regulation and the discovery of sensitive environmental problems. But perceived risks can often be turned to the advantage of both developers and society when improved environmental performance goes hand in hand with increased operating efficiency—as it can in water, energy, and transportation projects (chapter 5). To realize this potential for mutual benefit, regulators must be clear about the performance standards the project sponsors must meet and allow them sufficient flexibility in operations.

In most countries many people, both poor and nonpoor, lack access to electricity, telephones, and piped water supply. Often they end up paying much higher prices for these services from alternative sources, such as for water from vendors. Many societies have made ensuring minimum access to basic services a policy

---

Box 1.8 Involving the private sector in resettlement

Where truly voluntary resettlement occurs—when land is purchased through fair negotiations—the private sponsors of the project can take the lead in addressing the issues. But where involuntary resettlement is necessary, the relationship between the government and the private sponsors is often antagonistic. Private sponsors will be unwilling to commit significant new investment because of the uncertainties in project design and timetables. Governments may offer to undertake the resettlement and even offer financial compensation in the event of delays. But such commitments are not always credible, at least in part because the government actions will be subject to international scrutiny.

Close public-private collaboration may offer the way to more humane resettlement at lower cost and in less time. The private sector can play an important supporting role, although the government must be prepared to take the lead. The government must set up the consultative process and the guidelines to ensure fair compensation for those to be resettled and to protect their livelihood. But once such guidelines are in place, the private project sponsors can work alongside government agencies in implementing resettlement—designing and developing new sites and offering the people affected work on the project and in spin-offs.

Source: Gentry in this volume.

---

objective, especially middle-income countries approaching universal access. This often implies subsidizing access for some of the poor, potentially jeopardizing the commercial viability of service supply. Economists generally agree that the best approach for achieving minimum access while safeguarding commercial viability is to provide an explicit subsidy for targeted households. A common practice under Argentine water contracts, for example, is to bill fully for services, but to have households pay only part of the bill and charge the government directly for the subsidized portion. In Chile the subsidies for rural electrification are built into contracts that are then competitively bid.

Issues relating to sector regulation, contracting, resettlement, the environment, and reaching the poor converge in the water supply sector. Few deals in water supply have been finalized in East Asia outside of Malaysia, but conference participants showed much interest in the sector. Because of the complexity of the issues in the water and sanitation sector, it is an important new frontier for public-private partnership in the region (box 1.9).

Box 1.9 Water supply and sanitation—regulation, the environment, and the poor

Because water is a basic necessity and clean water is required to prevent the spread of disease, universal access to affordable water is a high priority everywhere. But throughout East Asia water supply systems are under great stress as rapidly growing urban populations place increasing demands on them. Perversely, in many systems subsidies have limited the expansion of supply while failing to benefit the poor, many of whom lack access to the public system and buy water at high prices from private vendors. Sewerage systems are even less developed, and service prices are much too low to cover the substantial investments required. As a consequence, poor sanitation is a growing threat to public health and the environment in many countries.

Private entry into water and sanitation has been constrained by system inefficiencies, uneconomic pricing, and governments' reluctance to award monopoly distribution rights in such a sensitive sector. Some contracts have been awarded to private operators—a water and sewerage contract in Manila, a sewerage contract in Malaysia, a management contract for the water distribution system in Macao, water sourcing and treatment contracts in Malaysia and Thailand. Similar contracts are under discussion in Chinese and Indonesian cities. But the needs extend well beyond these early efforts.

Regulating the water and sanitation sector is a challenge, because large investment requirements and high environmental standards imply a need for long-run price increases. Balancing the goals of expanding access, including to the poor, protecting the environment, and preventing abuse of monopoly rights creates a policy challenge that can be met only through increased experience and public-private collaboration.

Capital markets and domestic finance for private infrastructure

In most East Asian economies the bulk of finance for private infrastructure has come from foreign sources. Yet most of the revenues from infrastructure projects are in domestic currency, raising the risk of currency devaluation and foreign exchange inconvertibility for foreign investors. The risks for foreign finance of private infrastructure increase the importance of domestic finance. But only about a quarter of the finance for private infrastructure in East Asia comes from domestic sources.

Why has there been so little domestic financing for private infrastructure? The low levels in East Asia today are not without historical precedent. Much of the financing for some of the infrastructure developed in North and South America in the nineteenth century came from the capital markets of the United Kingdom (Eichengreen 1996). But domestic savings in the recipient countries were low. By contrast, East Asian economies have some of the highest savings rates ever recorded (figure 1.5). Total savings are running at 30–35 percent of gross domestic product (GDP), and private savings at 25–30 percent. Moreover, a significant share of the savings is going into financial assets, with bank credit, for example, comparable to levels in some industrial countries (figure 1.6).

So the issue is clearly not a lack of domestic resources. Even if the private sector's share in infrastructure investment in East Asia reaches 30 percent in the next few years and more than 50 percent by early in the next century, it would still amount to only 2–5 percent of GDP, a small fraction of private domestic savings. Instead, the low domestic financing for private infrastructure stems from a combination of relatively immature domestic capital markets, especially bond markets, and domestic investors' cautiousness about such investments. Apparently, domestic investors are more averse to the risks associated with the present phase of infrastruc-

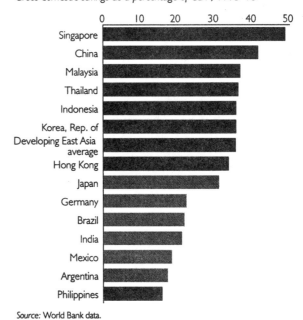

Figure 1.5 East Asia has extraordinarily high savings . . .
Gross domestic savings as a percentage of GDP, 1993–95

Source: World Bank data.

Figure 1.6 ... much of it channeled into financial investment
Total credit provided by the banking sector as a percentage of GDP, 1995

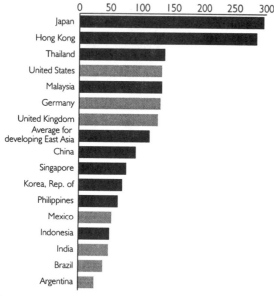

Source: World Bank data.

ture investment than are foreign investors, who have greater opportunities for diversification. In the coming years use of domestic equity markets is likely to grow rapidly, but long-term domestic debt finance will probably lag in most countries, taking off only when domestic contractual savings become significant, as has occurred to some extent in Malaysia. (Contractual savings have also been used in Singapore, but in a predominantly public sector context.)

Equity markets

Despite East Asia's gradual approach to privatization of state-owned utilities, almost $11 billion was raised on foreign and domestic stock markets in 1989–95 (compared with $28 billion in Latin America), almost entirely for power, trans-

port, and telecommunications (table 1.2). For example, PT Telkom, the Indonesian telecommunications company, went to the market with an initial public offering in November 1995 and raised $1.69 billion, mainly onshore, on the Jakarta and Surabaya stock exchanges and later raised some $600 million through an onshore private placement. The private Indonesian toll road company, Citra Marga Nusphala Persada, also has raised some $600 million on local stock markets. But with foreign investors accounting for almost 80 percent of trading on the Jakarta exchange, and about 50 percent in Bangkok, Kuala Lumpur, and Manila, the estimate of onshore finance includes a large share of foreign financing.

Stock markets are likely to become an important source of finance for infrastructure companies in East Asia. Although the depth and institutional framework of the region's exchanges are less well developed than those of mature exchanges, stock markets throughout the region are growing and deepening fast. By one estimate the Kuala Lumpur exchange saw a doubling in efficiency between 1992 and 1996, and the Jakarta exchange improved nearly as fast (World Bank 1997c).

Although East Asia's stock markets are still young, capitalization in several is comparable to or greater than that in rich countries—and is growing fast (figure 1.7). Stock market capitalization in Hong Kong (China), Malaysia, and Singapore was more than 200 percent of GDP in 1995—substantially greater than in the United Kingdom and the United States. The exchanges in Thailand and the Philippines also had high levels of capitalization (though Thailand's has since fallen back). Finance from stock markets will, of course, depend on the perceived riski-

Table 1.2 Equity market financing of infrastructure privatization in East Asia and Latin America, 1989–95
(US$ billions)

Sector	East Asia			Latin America		
	Onshore	Offshore	Total	Onshore	Offshore	Total
Transportation	2.2	1.2	3.4	3.1	0.9	4.0
Telecommunications	1.7	2.2	3.9	4.3	11.4	15.7
Power	2.5	0.9	3.4	3.9	4.4	8.2
Other	0.1	0.1	0.2	0.1	0.0	0.1
Total	6.5	4.3	10.9	11.3	16.7	28.0

Note: Data may not add to totals because of rounding.
Source: World Bank, International Economics Department, Privatization Database.

Figure 1.7 Stock market capitalization in several East Asian economies is high and growing fast . . .

Stock market capitalization as a percentage of GDP, 1990 and 1995

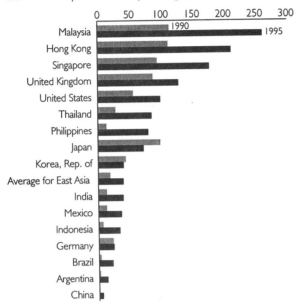

Source: International Finance Corporation and World Bank data; Claessens and Glaessner forthcoming.

Figure 1.8 . . . but bond markets are still relatively underdeveloped in most of the region

Bond market capitalization as a percentage of GDP, 1990 and 1994

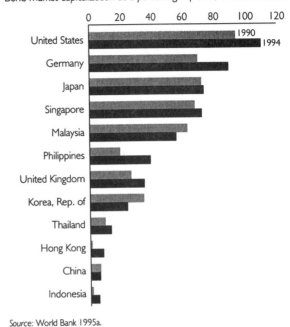

Source: World Bank 1995a.

ness of projects. In mid-1997 Malaysian investors showed signs of caution over some infrastructure projects: a June 1997 rights issue for the finance of the 2,400-megawatt Bakun Dam was reported to be 63 percent undersubscribed (*Financial Times*, June 12, 1997).

A relatively new development is the raising of funds through securities backed by pooled infrastructure assets. Several Chinese projects issued such securities to raise financing on the Hong Kong (China) and the domestic Shenzhen stock exchanges. For example, in 1996 the Guangdong Provincial Expressway Company raised HK$477.9 million (US$62 million) through an issue of B shares on the Shenzhen exchange, backed by stakes in completed revenue-generating toll projects, including the Jujiang Bridge and Guangzhou-Foshan expressway. The money raised was used to finance additional investment. In late 1996 the Anhui Expressway Company raised $100 million on the Hong Kong (China) exchange to finance three highway projects, with the company's balance sheet secured by the Hening Expressway, already in operation (World Bank 1997a). This use of assets (originally financed by public or private equity or debt finance) to raise resources

on local and international capital markets to finance additional investments could emerge as a significant pattern.

Debt finance and bond markets

While there has been significant activity on East Asia's domestic equity markets (though much of it involving foreign investors), domestic debt finance of private infrastructure has been relatively limited. Does this reflect failure by the domestic financial system to efficiently intermediate private savings into profitable investment opportunities? The answer is yes, but the problem relates to the current phase of financial market development rather than short-run policy. Banks still dominate East Asian financial systems and account for the bulk of private savings in financial instruments. Deposits are mainly short to medium term, limiting banks' ability to make the long-term investments typical in infrastructure projects. East Asian banks also have less capacity to support large-scale projects than do the much larger and financially stronger international banks.

Financing infrastructure through long-term bonds is an attractive option in principle. Bond

---

Box 1.10 Contractual savings in long-run finance for infrastructure

Chile. Chile's independent pension funds have become major players in domestic infrastructure finance, through purchases of both bonds and equity. Since they were privatized, the funds have channeled some $4.8 billion into electricity and gas distributors and $1.6 billion into telecommunications companies and are becoming increasingly involved in transportation.

Malaysia. The first independent power project awarded in Malaysia, the YTL power generation project, was financed entirely in local markets, including through a 1.5 billion ringgit (RM) (almost $500 million), ten-year bond subscribed by the Employee Provident Fund and a RM 1.6 billion floating rate loan underwritten by local banks to finance construction. Subsequent projects using bond finance have included other power projects (Lumut Power) and transport projects (the North-South Expressway). The Employee Provident Fund has been active in most of these bond issues.

The Netherlands. The Wijkertunnel was the first project in continental Europe to be financed through domestic markets. It raised most of the tunnel's $342 million cost through private placement of bonds with Dutch insurance and pension funds (the Netherlands is unusual in Europe in having fully funded pension schemes).

The United Kingdom. The First Hydro project involved the first-ever use of a sterling eurobond issue for project finance. This hydroelectric plant was bought by Mission Energy in 1995 and refinanced through issuance of £400 million of 25.5-year eurobonds. Most of the bonds were purchased by British insurance companies.

The United States. The Independence Funding Corporation, which owns a 1,000-megawatt gas-fired cogeneration plant in New York State, was the first independent power producer in the world to receive an investment-grade rating and obtain finance through the capital markets. Backed by strong power offtake agreements, its successful offering in 1993 of secured notes totaling $717 million was purchased mainly by U.S. institutional investors. In 1995 California Energy issued the first below-investment-grade bonds, in the form of eight-year limited recourse notes secured on the cash flow and assets of Salton Sea power projects; Salton Sea Funding Corporation subsequently placed $475 million of investment-grade nonrecourse project bonds with U.S. institutional investors.

Source: World Bank 1997a.

---

markets were an important source of finance in earlier eras of private infrastructure, notably in the building of transport networks in North and South America (see Eichengreen 1996). In the more recent past bond finance was used primarily by state corporations—as in French power investments and the U.S. Tennessee Valley Authority. In Indonesia the state-owned power company Perusahaan Listrik Negara (PLN) has similarly made use of the local bond market, becoming one of the major market players. It made its first bond offering in 1992, of 300 billion rupiah (Rp), and issued another Rp 2.6 trillion at the end of 1996, mainly of five- to seven-year maturities. In general, however, bond markets in East Asia are relatively undeveloped, with turnover much lower than in the developed markets of industrial economies (figure 1.8).

The use of bonds in limited recourse project finance has emerged in recent years. The issues have been placed in relatively well-developed financial markets, primarily the U.S. 144a market (which permits resale of purchased securities to qualified investors). Institutional investors, primarily insurance companies and pension funds have been the major purchasers of these bonds (box 1.10). Because institutional investors manage contractual savings with long maturities, long-gestation infrastructure projects are potentially attractive investment opportunities as long as risks are adequately addressed.

Most developing countries have a relatively small pool of institutional investors, however. Two of the exceptions are Chile and Malaysia. In both countries pension funds have played an important part in infrastructure finance, although under very different market conditions. In Chile pension funds are private and autonomous, and they compete for resources from individual workers, though within fairly narrow limits. The government has steadily broadened the range of assets that pension funds may purchase. In Malaysia there is much greater state involvement in the economy, and the Employee Provident Fund is a public entity with relatively restricted investment options. Until recently the fund held the bulk of its investment in government bonds (and still holds about half in this instrument), but it is now pursuing a more diversified investment policy.

Bond markets in East Asia are relatively underdeveloped in part because of the relatively low issuance of government bonds, which usually provide the core of the bond market. The low bond issues in turn stem from the low levels of deficit finance. Underdeveloped bond markets also reflect the relatively limited use of external finance by the corporate sector, owing to the dominance of family firms. Bond markets are certainly growing in importance, and the institutional framework is likely to improve rapidly, as it did for equity markets, with the development of benchmarks, improved settlement and clearance procedures, and an information infrastructure (World Bank 1995a).

As emphasized throughout this volume, however, infrastructure investments continue to involve significant risks, a concern for investors looking for the relatively moderate but secure returns characteristic of bond markets. Experience suggests the need for caution in forcing the pace: many technically autonomous public pension funds in Latin America saw a substantial share of their investments channeled into low-return activities. More important is to reduce the risks faced by infrastructure projects and to foster the development of genuinely autonomous contractual savings institutions that will make prudent decisions on purchases of infrastructure bonds and other savings instruments. With further pension reforms likely in East Asia and great potential for growth in life insurance, large growth can be expected in the savings available for long-term investment. But this growth will not happen overnight.

A framework for moving forward

There is no magic formula for accelerating private sector involvement in infrastructure, but there is a set of common principles for fostering such involvement while achieving efficiency gains and meeting societal goals. These principles—transparent processes, stable rules, price reforms, maximum competition, and incentive-based regulatory structures—are the pillars of a basic framework that each country can customize to fit its priorities and institutions. Developing effective frameworks for private participation will be an evolutionary process as countries learn from their experience. But systematic sharing of information among East Asian economies and with other countries at all stages of development will speed this process. It may

also enable late starters to skip the learning-by-doing phase, jumping directly to deeper reforms and the gains they bring in efficiency, investment growth, finance, and public confidence.

The Jakarta dialogue and other public-private forums organized by the World Bank confirm that while private participation in infrastructure is new and the issues complex, a rich body of experience is fast developing. This experience reveals major differences between sectors and countries, suggesting that no one model is universally applicable. Yet the discussions between policymakers and private executives have identified common principles and strategies that can help countries shorten the learning curve and develop more effective ways to promote private participation (Kohli 1997).

Among the lessons that have emerged from such discussions are the preconditions needed to ensure the sustainability of large-scale private investments in infrastructure:

- Projects must produce services at prices the public is willing to pay.
- Where government subsidies or other forms of support are essential, they should be transparent and sustainable.
- Private projects must be bankable, that is, their financial returns must be commensurate with the risks perceived by private investors and financiers.

To meet these preconditions, most countries need to undertake far-reaching policy and institutional reforms to improve the financial viability and profits of infrastructure projects, increase competition and transparency in contracting, and reduce the risks of investing in the sector. Such reforms build credibility with both the general public and private investors.

The goals set for private participation frameworks vary among countries and sectors and continue to evolve. But they are likely to include:

- Price reforms that ensure sustainable revenues and reduce future price uncertainties.
- A more transparent and credible regulatory and legal framework.
- Greater competition (including the breakup of monopolies, whether public or private).
- Direct relations between the ultimate consumers and suppliers to enhance accountability.

Box 1.11 The role of multilateral agencies in promoting private participation in infrastructure

Many participants at the Jakarta seminar believed that the World Bank and other multilateral institutions also have a crucial role to play in bringing about a sharp increase in private participation. They proposed that this role focus on:

- Supporting continued public-private dialogue at both the country and the regional level.
- Sharing information and lessons of experience from within and outside the region.
- Helping countries develop a more conducive framework for private participation.
- Formulating standards for bidding and contractual documents.
- Supporting the development of new financing mechanisms and the design of a policy framework for domestic financial sector development, including bond markets.
- Financing more privately sponsored projects in a way that maximizes the leveraging of Bank commitments.

- Separation of sovereign and commercial risks to allocate risks efficiently.
- The development of domestic capital markets and of mechanisms to facilitate provision of long-term debt, including the creation of fixed income securities and bond markets.

Most developing economies in the region are addressing many of these constraints and issues. But almost all are focusing on the needs of a few projects or sectors, addressing only some of the cross-sectoral issues, and pursuing reforms more slowly than desirable. At this pace and intensity, developing a robust and complete framework will take a long time, delaying the full gains from private participation.

The high-level dialogue at Jakarta and at regional political forums offers a potential platform for launching a comprehensive initiative aimed at developing a complete framework in all the region's developing economies within a similar timeframe. Such a regionwide initiative is essential if the target of a 30 percent or greater private sector share in infrastructure investment is to be met by the end of this century.

To achieve this target, countries need to formulate (or clarify) their objectives, strategies, and priorities for private participation. They need to streamline internal decisionmaking, develop a

framework for mitigating and sharing risk, and put in place policies and procedures for transparent and competitive bidding and contracting in order to take advantage of competitive market forces and reduce transaction costs. And they need to redouble efforts to develop domestic bond markets and financial instruments to support long-term investment in infrastructure projects.

Regional sharing of information and other forms of cooperation could contribute much to the initiative. As the trade liberalization initiative of Asia-Pacific Economic Cooperation (APEC) showed, when economies take parallel or complementary actions in a policy area they create important synergies and momentum, and multicountry initiatives yield economies of scale. To help maximize the benefits for reforming economies, countries with more developed markets could take steps to promote a greater flow of private investment and management skills across the region.

Five sets of actions across the Asia-Pacific region would help create these important synergies and ensure the full benefits of the reforms for all economies in the region:

- Reorient policies and practices of export credit and official development agencies to directly support private projects. In some cases this may require increasing the resources available to these agencies. The Japanese government has recently made a policy decision to provide greater support to private financing of infrastructure projects in East Asia and has asked the Japanese Export-Import Bank and Overseas Economic Cooperation Fund to reflect this decision in their operating strategies. Other industrial economies could take similar steps.
- Provide a larger volume of political risk insurance to viable private investments. As the Japanese government has recently suggested, there is also a need to multi-source insurance and export credit, with greater involvement of agencies from the more advanced developing countries.
- Remove regulatory barriers and other disincentives to investment by infrastructure providers and institutional investors in the region in otherwise creditworthy infrastructure projects.

- Provide more technical assistance (through grant funds and expertise) to the developing economies for policy reforms and institutional development.
- Share information and lessons of experience in both industrial and developing economies and foster public-private dialogue through the regional forums—APEC, the Association of South-East Asian Nations (ASEAN), and the Asia, Europe, and Mediterranean (ASEM) association.

What follows

The chapters in this volume discuss the issues of private provision of infrastructure from the perspective of practitioners and policymakers deeply engaged in them. Chapter 2, by Don Russell, describes the experience of Australia in designing a reform strategy and making the transition from an incremental, project-specific approach to more ambitious structural change. This experience shows how a move to sector-wide reform, with broad competition and clear rules of the game, can reduce the need for project-specific guarantees and stimulate active interest among private investors, with substantial gains for the treasury.

Chapter 3, by Yahya Yaacob and G. Naidu, uses the experience of Malaysia as the basis for a discussion of the choices and tradeoffs in different methods of contracting with the private sector. Contracting has become a central feature of the current phase in private delivery of infrastructure and will always be important in areas where a competitive model of delivery is not feasible. Malaysia has pursued a relatively managed approach to contracting, in contrast to the competitive model increasingly used in other countries.

The Chilean experience, discussed in chapter 4 by Alejandro Jadresic, demonstrates the central importance of a regulatory structure and the commitment required to establish such a structure. Like Australia, Chile has been able to curtail government guarantees by creating regulated markets in which contracting parties reach outcomes in line with commercial principles. The chapter also discusses how Chile has dealt with major societal concerns, including

environmental issues and the provision of infrastructure services to the poor.

The discussion on regulation is continued in a thematic chapter by Bradford Gentry on environmental and resettlement issues in infrastructure projects (chapter 5). These issues are clearly of great importance to society, and they have also become key risk factors for private developers and investors. The chapter shows that it is best to make resolving environmental and resettlement concerns an integral part of the project cycle. The final chapter, by Montek Ahluwalia, discusses a broad range of financing questions, focusing on risks associated with infrastructure provision and drawing especially on examples from India.

Notes

1. The focus here is on international financing because consistent data across countries and over time have recently become available, while comparable data on domestic financing of infrastructure are not yet available. The reader is thus cautioned that the picture presented is incomplete. While the intercountry comparisons and trends are broadly indicative of overall financing patterns, they may be less useful for countries such as Malaysia and Thailand, where there has been significant domestic financing of infrastructure.

2. The data here on international infrastructure financing cover closed and signed transactions of international loans and bond and equity issues reported by capital market sources. The data have been provided by the World Bank's International Economics Department.

3. This section draws on World Bank 1996.

References

Claessens, Constantijn, and Thomas Glaessner. Forthcoming. *Are Financial Sector Weaknesses Undermining the East Asian Miracle?* Directions in Development Series. Washington, D.C.: World Bank.

Eichengreen, Barry. 1996. "Financing Infrastructure in Developing Countries: Lessons from the Railway Age." In Ashoka Mody, ed., *Infrastructure Delivery: Private Initiative and the Public Good*. EDI Development Studies. Washington, D.C.: World Bank.

Kohli, Harinder. 1997. "Developing Infrastructure for the New East Asia: Forging a Public-Private Partnership." In Lionel Walsh, Robert Taylor, and Ron Katz, eds., *Building the New Asia*. Paris: International Chamber of Commerce.

Kwong, Sunny Kai-Sun. 1997. "Hong Kong: Private Participation with Strong Government Control." In Ashoka Mody, ed., *Infrastructure Strategies in East Asia: The Untold Story.* Washington, D.C.: Economic Development Institute, World Bank.

Mikesell, Deborah Newitter. 1997. "The Range of Private Investment in Infrastructure." Infrastructure Working Group Background Paper. World Bank, Development Economics Vice Presidency, Washington, D.C.

Naidu, G., and Cassey Lee. 1997. "Malaysia: The Transition to Privatization." In Ashoka Mody, ed., *Infrastructure Strategies in East Asia: The Untold Story.* Washington, D.C.: Economic Development Institute, World Bank.

Philippines, Department of Finance. 1995. "New Policy on Guarantees for Private Infrastructure Projects: A Consultative Document." Manila.

Smith, Warrick, and Michael Klein. 1994. "Infrastructure Regulation: Issues and Options for East Asia." World Bank, Private Sector Development Department, Washington, D.C.

World Bank. 1994. *World Development Report 1994: Infrastructure for Development.* New York: Oxford University Press.

———. 1995a. *The Emerging Asian Bond Market.* Washington, D.C.

———. 1995b. "Infrastructure Development in East Asia and Pacific: Toward a New Public-Private Partnership." East Asia and Pacific, Office of the Vice President, Washington, D.C.

———. 1996. "Frontiers of the Public-Private Interface in East Asia's Infrastructure." East Asia and Pacific Regional Office, Washington, D.C.

———. 1997a. "China: Mobilizing Domestic Capital Markets for Infrastructure Financing." Report 16637-CHA. East Asia and Pacific, Country Department II, Washington, D.C.

———. 1997b. *Global Development Finance 1997.* Washington, D.C.

———. 1997c. *Private Capital Flows to Developing Countries: The Path to Financial Integration.* New York: Oxford University Press.

———. 1997d. *World Development Indicators 1997.* Washington, D.C.

CHAPTER 2

Organizing the Government for Efficient Private Participation in Infrastructure: Lessons from Australia

Don Russell

Unmet infrastructure needs in East Asia are constraining both economic growth and social development. Although spending on infrastructure has increased sharply in recent decades, it has not kept pace with demand. Investment in infrastructure rose from 3.6 percent of gross domestic product (GDP) in the 1970s to about 4.6 percent of GDP in the 1980s and to about 5.0–5.5 percent of GDP in 1993, when it reached $70 billion. But to meet investment requirements —estimated at $1.3–$1.5 billion between 1995 and 2004—the investment to GDP ratio will have to rise to 6.5–7 percent. Past methods of funding infrastructure, which depended heavily on export credit organizations, multilateral lending institutions, and aid agencies, will not be able to fund the required growth. Nor will governments in the region be able to raise the necessary funds through tax revenues, borrowing, or increasing revenues of public utilities.

Given these massive investment needs and the inability of East Asian countries to finance the needs themselves, it is natural that they would look to the private sector to provide capital. But experience with the private sector has failed to meet expectations, raising doubts about whether it can participate in infrastructure development in a way that leaves countries and their communities better off than they otherwise would have been.

"The original high expectations of the host countries and of private sponsors have not been met" and "neither the governments nor private sector are satisfied with progress," according to the World Bank (1995). What went wrong?

Experience in the region points to two main problems. First, involving the private sector in infrastructure is more complex than originally thought and requires a level of sophistication on the part of government that takes time and experience to develop. Second, notwithstanding the stated intention of all governments to involve the private sector in infrastructure, many governments are still working through what form that involvement should take or have reservations about the appropriateness of private sector involvement. Such ambiguity and ambivalence on the part of government can cloud the true nature of the risks associated with any infrastructure project and lead to long delays in getting governments to make key decisions.

This chapter looks at the role of government in involving the private sector in infrastructure development. It draws on experience in the region, particularly in Australia, to set guidelines for government processes and organization.

Australia's experience with infrastructure provides some interesting insights. During the 1960s Australia invested 9 percent of GDP in infrastructure—almost all of it publicly funded —to meet the postwar surge in immigration. Since then the figure has fallen to 6 percent as a result of a sharp cutback in government funding, but private infrastructure has expanded substantially and now accounts for about 20 percent of total investment. Financial closings worth $4 billion in private infrastructure were signed in 1995, representing 80 percent of private investment in infrastructure in East Asia.

Australia's involvement with private infrastructure began around 1987. The federal government created an environment that encouraged development of private infrastructure, but complex federal-state issues have meant that progress has not been guided by a blueprint from Canberra. Many lessons have been learned from this process, and a large private infrastructure industry has developed in Australia, backed by a range of institutional investors. Australian design and construction companies, law firms, and investment banks have expanded and used their experience to build businesses in East Asia.

The chapter is organized as follows. The first section lays out the complex issues involved in private infrastructure and shows why government commitment is so important. The second section examines the competing interests of the various government agencies involved in private projects and considers the implications for private infrastructure. The third section shows how governments try to resolve the problems raised by the complexity of the issues and the large number of agencies involved, and the fourth section suggest how governments might reorganize to improve private-public cooperation and ensure that they obtain the best possible deals. The last section draws lessons from the Australian experience.

Recognizing the importance of government commitment

Key decisionmakers in the public sector must be convinced that private provision of infrastructure makes sense, and they must be willing to follow through on that commitment. Without such commitment the contribution of private infrastructure to the burgeoning infrastructure needs of East Asia will be only marginal. Companies involved in the private infrastructure industry typically look for evidence of commitment in the following forms:

- Willingness of senior ministers and leaders to be involved in resolving conflicts affecting projects.
- Clear signals to government officials, including officials of public utilities, that the leadership wants particular projects to be successfully negotiated (although not necessarily to the advantage of particular companies).
- Willingness to follow through on other policy matters that flow from particular private projects, such as sectoral plans or frame-

works that give structure to particular projects and reduce risk.
- Willingness to put in place the distribution facilities necessary for a private project to succeed. This is particularly important in countries in which private interests are not permitted to own distribution facilities.
- A track record of success.

Companies look for commitment from government within both the narrow context of formal project negotiations and the wider context of private infrastructure policy.

Paradoxically, although the private sector is providing a growing share of infrastructure investment, the government's responsibility for guiding the process may be greater than it was when the system was exclusively public. This increased responsibility stems from the fact that adding a private component to the system makes the system more complex and hence requires more sophisticated government management.

Variations in the relationship between the public and private sectors

Private infrastructure projects invariably involve governments at the planning, construction, and operating stages. If a project is part of a broader public system, such as a toll road, a water treatment facility, or an electricity generator, some public utility or authority will expect the new facility to fit comfortably within its systems and planning arrangements. There will be pressure to use similar equipment, compatible technology, and existing contractors and to maximize the value of the public network (existing or planned). From the outset tension will exist regarding the exact nature of private sector involvement.

At one extreme the project may be a disguised financing arrangement designed to extend a public network without appearing to add to public sector liabilities. In such arrangements the public sector bears all the commercial risk and guarantees that the revenue connected to the project will cover the bondholders who finance it. The private sector is responsible for the design and construction of the project and for the financing arrangements, which often must be innovative if financing is to extend beyond fifteen years. The public sector seeks to have the project built and off its balance sheet to avoid the appearance of incurring new liabilities. If the public sector cannot borrow, it seeks to get the project built as cheaply as possible. If the private project is privately operated, there is the potential for operating efficiencies and "benchmarking" of other parts of the public network, something that is often attractive to public sector managers. At the other extreme, a project can be completely commercial, with the equity holders bearing full risk and bondholders or commercial banks receiving no guarantees. Output carries a market-determined price, and equity holders can reap large returns if the project is successful or lose their investment if the project fails. In between these two extremes there is scope for different kinds of guarantees and allocation of risk between the government and the private sector.

The importance of the government's role cannot be overstated. The government determines the exact nature of the project and must be very clear about what it is trying to achieve in order to prevent confusion and frustration on all sides. If, for example, the government wants to negotiate a deal that is really a disguised financing arrangement but is loathe to provide guarantees out of concern over its credit standing in the eyes of the international rating agencies, it cannot expect to negotiate narrow margins on the financing. Similarly, friction and costly delay will ensue if private sponsors want to maintain full commercial control of a project while the government wants it to be part of an existing public network.

The nature of the government's commitment

Governments need to commit both to the concept of private infrastructure and to individual projects. Without a strategy on private sector participation, negotiations over individual projects will bog down in confusion. Without a government commitment to individual projects that fit into the broader strategy, private sponsors will be unable to wade through the government approval processes.

Negotiations over a take-or-pay contract, for example, will normally be complex and drawn out. Such contracts are used when private infra-

structure augments a public utility network. In such circumstances the public utility purchases the output of the private project. The viability and attractiveness of the project will be determined by the nature and robustness of the contractual relationship between the project and the government, and enormous effort will go into negotiating this contract.

All investment decisions by the private sector involve government approval processes to some extent, but private infrastructure projects are in a class of their own because of their long lives, their potential for abuse of market power, and the long tradition in many countries of utilities serving a social as well as an economic function. The private sector will have to comply with a wide range of government approval procedures, involving foreign investment regulations and exchange controls, export and import controls, environment and zoning regulations, the sourcing of equipment and other inputs, and local employment requirements.

Case studies from Australia

The Australian experience illustrates the importance of government commitment and the way government commitment develops. In the mid-1980s Australia went through a process of economic adjustment, brought about by the need to internationalize the economy and cut back on overseas borrowings. The federal government reduced government outlays to create a budget surplus and cut back on the ability of state governments to borrow. As a result both state governments and the federal government found it difficult to fund new infrastructure projects. As the 1980s progressed, the need to finance new infrastructure became more pressing, and the federal government created a framework within which the private sector could fund projects viewed as commercially viable. Part of this framework provided for the privatization of government assets at both the federal and state levels. Cutbacks in federal government funding put pressure on the states to run their government enterprises and utilities efficiently and to consider selling assets.

The federal government went out of its way to facilitate private involvement in infrastructure and the privatization of assets through a range of incentives. It had no direct control over how states took advantage of the changed environment, however, and each state approached the task differently and with different motives. As a result Australia has experienced a wide range of outcomes with private infrastructure since 1987, when the process first gained momentum:

- Negotiations over a take-or-pay contract for an electricity generator at Loy Yang B in Victoria were drawn out and very expensive.
- Construction of a 600-megawatt power station in Collie in Western Australia was canceled after lengthy negotiations with private consortia.
- Private toll roads were constructed in New South Wales and Victoria.
- Water treatment facilities in New South Wales and Victoria were constructed, and more such projects are under consideration in South Australia.
- A tunnel under Sydney Harbour was constructed in a deal that appears to have been close to a disguised financing transaction.

Australia has also seen the development of a range of clear policy structures that have evolved as a result of this diverse experience:

- Following the difficulties of the Loy Yang B negotiations, Victoria deregulated its power industry by separating and selling off generators and distributors. The competitive framework has been so successful that Victoria has attracted a new range of long-term private investors willing to fund the electricity industry at very narrow margins and pay very high prices for assets.
- A national electricity grid is in train that will lead to the competitive supply of electricity across states. Third-party access arrangements are being put in place to facilitate development of a national gas market.
- State government utilities will be brought under the authority of the national competition regulator, which will prevent them from serving as revenue-raising devices for state governments and force them to compete.
- Governments have created an investment climate that is now sufficiently attractive and stable for investment banks and other institutions to set up private infrastructure funds to channel long-term finance into infrastructure projects.
- A framework for involving the private sector in water has been developed in South Australia that keeps rates under government control but has the private sector managing the system.

Involving the private sector in the power industry. In 1991 the government of Victoria decided to sell the unfinished Loy Yang B power station and commenced negotiations with Mission Energy, the entity Southern California Edison uses to conduct business outside its traditional operations in the United States. Severe budgetary difficulties brought about by extensive losses sustained by its government-owned bank, the State Bank of Victoria, and other pressures meant that the state government was unable to fund completion of the power station. Partial sale of the unfinished power station was seen as the only way of completing construction. Selling Loy Yang B to a private operator and benchmarking other generators against its performance was expected to raise efficiency and improve industrial relations at other generators in the La Trobe Valley. In fact, industrial relations did improve dramatically, and the introduction of a private operator enabled the industry to revise consumer pricing to better reflect costs.

Sale of the plant was legally complex and expensive, and the scope for misunderstanding and suspicion was broad. The sale was completed by a new state government, elected in 1992, that accepted the basic approach of the previous government although it allowed Mission Energy to purchase 51 percent instead of the 40 percent offered by the previous government (box 2.1).

The sale of Loy Yang B was completed while the newly elected state government was in the initial stages of deregulating the electricity industry, which could have involved the breaking up or privatization of the state-owned power utility, the State Electricity Commission of Victoria. Some flexibility in the take-or-pay contract was necessary to allow for future deregulation, a development that concerned Mission Energy and terrified the Australian banks. In the end the contract was signed and the sale was

Box 2.1 Allocating risks in the sale of Loy Yang B

Loy Yang B is a 1,000-megawatt plant made up of two 500-megawatt units. The state government of Victoria offered for sale a 51 percent share of a A$2.4 billion asset. The authorities had to recover the cost of the plant's construction, and bidding took place on the basis of the electricity tariff. The authorities entered into a thirty-three-year take-or-pay contract; financing was arranged by a consortium of institutions led by two Australian banks. The take-or-pay contract involved a capability charge to cover fixed costs and an energy charge to cover variable costs, such as coal and water. The security of the financing rested on the perceived security of the take-or-pay contract, and the banks examined that contract carefully.

The state government utility, the State Electricity Commission of Victoria (SECV), took on the construction risk of completing the power station. The SECV was able to lock in the electricity tariff for ten years by hedging its power price through interest rate swaps to cover changes to the capability charge brought about by fluctuations in interest rates.

The purchaser, Mission Energy, reportedly incurred costs of about A$50 million negotiating the purchase. The costs of the sale to the state of Victoria were estimated by the state auditor-general at A$86.7 million.

Cost of sale of Loy Yang B to state government

	Amount (A$ millions)
Costs to the SECV	
Legal and other costs	23.2
Forgone delayed settlement	7.6
Stamp duty paid on behalf of Mission Energy	6.2
Total cost to SECV	37.0
Costs to government	
Forgone stamp duty	49.7
Total	86.7

Note: A$1 = US$0.78.
Source: Victoria, Auditor-General 1994.

Box 2.2 Breaking up the electricity industry in Victoria and creating a competitive market for electricity

After the sale of Loy Yang B in December 1992 the Victorian government revamped the electricity industry, which now consists of the following components:
- Five competitive, independently operating generating companies (three brown coal, one gas, and one hydro), two of which have been sold and three of which are being prepared for sale.
- A publicly owned transmission company, Power Net Victoria, which owns and maintains the high-voltage grid.
- A power exchange, which uses the transmission grid and which is responsible for the wholesale market arranging dispatch and system security. The power exchange is not an arm of the generators, and the wholesale price of electricity varies.
- Five regionally based distribution businesses, which have an initial franchise (to be phased out by 2001) in respect of franchise customers but which are free to contest (along with independent retailers from other states) business within each other's region for nonfranchise customers. Under the current system nonfranchise customers are customers who use more than 750 megawatts a year and therefore are free to choose their distributor. Eventually all customers will have the right to choose their supplier.

completed, although the contract was lengthened considerably to build in flexibility. The Victorian government eventually broke up the electricity industry and put a competitive structure in place with industry-specific legislation (box 2.2). The sale of Loy Yang B to Mission Energy did not fit into the competitive structure subsequently established. By passing legislation, the Victorian government could easily have changed the nature of Mission Energy's investment. It chose not to do so, however, and the legislation effectively puts a fence around Loy Yang B. The importance of this decision by the Victorian government was not lost on the industry or the Australian banks that had fought so hard to obtain guarantees from the government covering the impact of deregulation in the final stages of the negotiations.

By its decision the Victorian government signaled that it was more interested in maintaining a good investment climate in Victoria than overriding the earlier agreement, even though that meant compromising on its competitive objectives. With a large privatization program at stake it was clear where the Victorian government thought its real interests lay.

Having watched this experience, the Australian banks are now less insistent on state guarantees, realizing that at the end of the day governments have considerable scope to act unilaterally and that a government's commitment to a policy framework is very important.

The difficult negotiations associated with the sale of Loy Yang B did not lead to the establishment of simpler processes for the construction of

Box 2.3 Mishandling award of the Collie power station contract

In 1989 the Western Australian government called for worldwide expressions of interest in building a 600-megawatt project on the Collie coal fields. The Collie proposal came from a plan drawn up in the 1970s as part of the long-term strategy of the vertically integrated public utility, the State Electricity Commission (SEC). Forty-four firms responded to the request for proposals and two final bidders—Asea Brown Boveri and a joint venture of Mitsubishi and Transfield, an Australian construction company—were selected.

In March 1991 Mitsubishi/Transfield was awarded the contract and set about creating a build-own-operate project. Westpac, an Australian bank, led the financing syndicate.

By April 1992 the first Collie proposal had fallen by the wayside, and Asea Brown Boveri (ABB) replaced Transfield/Mitsubishi, with ANZ Bank leading the financing syndicate. In September 1992 ABB submitted a new proposal that contained large cost increases and some conditions that were unacceptable to the government. In February 1993 a new state government was elected that continued to negotiate with ABB, with the power purchase agreement the main issue. Amid heated debate the new government canceled the Collie project in July 1993. In its place the government announced a plan for a 300-megawatt single unit power station that would be funded and owned by the SEC but operated by a private company.

Cancellation of the original 600-megawatt Collie project left the private sponsors bitter, although the decision to allow ABB to build the 300-megawatt plant went some way toward smoothing relations between ABB and the government.

Box 2.4 Letting the private sector manage a publicly owned water system in South Australia

The South Australian government sought private sector participation in the water industry in order to improve the efficiency of the industry and to build a competitive water industry in South Australia capable of winning contracts in East Asia.

The successful contractor, United Water, a consortium of Compagnie Generale des Eaux, Thames Water, and Kinhill Engineers of South Australia, committed itself to a 20 percent cost reduction and to A$628 million of exports to overseas and interstate markets for the ten years beginning in 1996. Under the terms of the 15.5-year contract, United Water manages, operates, and maintains the water and wastewater system for Adelaide, a city of 1.2 million. The government continues to own the assets and sets prices to customers. The government therefore continues to shoulder the responsibility of setting prices in a way that ensures that water is used efficiently.

The state utility, South Australian Water, will continue to provide the full range of water and wastewater services to the nonmetropolitan areas of South Australia; it is in the process of having ten BOT plants constructed for this purpose. United Water will manage the day-to-day operations of the water system, put together and manage the capital investment program, and make recommendations on how the capital program should be financed. Financing the program could involve new BOT schemes, but final decisions will be made by the minister and the state cabinet.

the Collie project in Western Australia (box 2.3). Unlike the Victorians, who concluded that it was important to establish a framework to guide private sector involvement, the West Australians approached Collie as a one-time set of negotiations. In the end the project was canceled.

The original proposal was recognized as having been too large. In addition, "the financiers were quite naive in dealing with Government . . . [and] seemed to be unaware of the process of government and the Parliament," according to the Western Australian minister for energy. The government was also critical of the escalating cost of the original contract and the structuring of the electricity price, which kept prices high until 2013, fourteen years after the plant started generating.

The banking industry rejected the claim that the banks had been unwilling to assume their

share of the risks, claiming that the cancellation of Collie was not a failure of the infrastructure industry but a failure for Australia. It called for greater transparency from government in the decisionmaking and tendering process.

The cancellation of Collie and the difficulties in negotiating the Loy Yang B deal have led to a general realization that large privately owned generators are difficult to incorporate into a vertically integrated publicly owned electricity system. To involve the private sector, governments need to be clear about what they are doing and identify the relationship they want the private generator to have with the public utility and with customers.

Outcomes in electricity have been quite different in Eastern and Western Australia. In the West cancellation of a build-own-operate scheme appears to have entrenched the power of the vertically integrated state utility. In the East breaking up the state utility into distribution and generating units and then selling them has been so successful that it has transformed the state's budgetary position and created a new industry structure with considerable potential for efficiency and lower energy prices. The challenge will be to keep competitive disciplines on the system and to prevent the distributors and generators from colluding. Speedy development of a competitive national grid will be very important. The success of the Victorian model has changed attitudes around the country and the vertically integrated power utility appears to be on the wane all over the country.

Involving the private sector in the water industry. The water industry has sought private capital both to provide the investment needed to extend and strengthen public networks and to increase efficiency by benchmarking of public facilities against private sector plants. Private investment has taken the form of build-own-operate (BOO) and build-operate-transfer (BOT) schemes, largely in New South Wales, Victoria, and nonmetropolitan South Australia (box 2.4). Most of the schemes have been closer to disguised financing arrangements than commercial businesses, and the auditor-general of New South Wales (1996) has suggested that the returns to the private equity holders are greater than warranted by the risk of the projects. The Prospect Water Filtration Plant, for example, is legally owned by the private sector, but it is constructed on land owned by Sydney Water, it is dependent on a supply of bulk water from Sydney Water, and Sydney Water is virtually its only customer. The private sector is able to recover from Sydney Water the entire debt and equity capital of the project in net present value terms, and the private sector's equity in the project is protected in the event of default. Public sector negotiators have gained more experience since the Prospect deal was signed, and recent projects have provided returns that are more compatible with the level of risk.

The South Australian government has used the private sector to increase efficiency and develop the water industry. It is the first state government to hand over management of the entire water supply of a capital city to a private contractor and allow the private sector to bear the risk of achieving performance targets.

At this stage there is little interest in Australia in selling franchises or handing water charging over to the private sector. There is enormous interest in using the private sector to manage water assets and build and own water treatment facilities integrated into a broader public system.

Involving the private sector in the transport sector. The Sydney Harbour Tunnel, construction of which began in 1988, was spurred by the federal government's curbing of state borrowings. The tunnel accelerated the development of a private infrastructure industry in Australia and was instrumental in ensuring that subsequent road projects allocated some risk to the private sector and were commercial. Today long-term institutional investors finance private toll roads, which are listed on the stock exchange.

Because of scrutiny by the auditor-general of New South Wales, the project is now seen as a disguised financing transaction in which the state bore all of the risks associated with traffic flow. The auditor-general (1994) has, in fact, concluded that for accounting purposes the tunnel is owned by the state government (box 2.5).

Several private toll roads have been constructed in Sydney and Melbourne (box 2.6), but policymakers now have reservations about the appropriateness of private sector involvement in this area.

Concerns center on the difficulty that the private sector has in handling network risk—a risk that the government is best suited to handle because of its planning responsibilities. After almost a decade Australian governments at the state and federal level are starting to crystallize their views on private involvement in transportation. There is broad agreement that there are important efficiency gains from having the private sector bear construction risk and manage state-owned assets, and a number of states have developed imaginative and useful models. One such model is for road maintenance. The New South Wales government's system of contracting road maintenance, which is based on achieving particular targets, is the first comprehensive system of its type in the world. Contracts will be specified in terms of the condition of the road assets over the term of the contract rather than in terms of the conventional

Box 2.5 Disguising a financing transaction as a commercial project: The Sydney Harbour Tunnel

Hailed as a commercial private sector project designed to relieve congestion on the Harbour Bridge when it commenced in January 1988, the Sydney Harbour Tunnel ended up as a disguised financing transaction of the New South Wales state government.

Finance for the tunnel was raised by the Sydney Harbour Tunnel Company, which issued bonds that were fully underwritten by the private sector. Responsibility for the bonds rests squarely with the state government, however, and revenues from tunnel tolls go to reducing the government's liability for the tunnel bonds. For this reason, the auditor-general of New South Wales (1994) concluded that for accounting purposes, the tunnel is owned by the Roads and Traffic Authority, a government authority. The tunnel toll does not cover the interest on the bonds, and the deficiency is covered by the toll on the Harbour Bridge and, in the first few years, by the state government. Under the original contract the Sydney Harbour Tunnel Company, which technically owns the tunnel, is entitled to a small return that is tied to its maintenance function. There is no effective return from operation of the tunnel.

The project grew out of federal government restrictions on state borrowing and the need to reduce congestion on the Harbour Bridge. It sparked the development of some innovative long-term (twenty-five-year) financing techniques and helped create a new market for institutional investment in private infrastructure.

Since the tunnel is effectively government owned, the state government will benefit from any increase in traffic volumes brought about by private investment in the Eastern Distributor, which connects with the tunnel.

Box 2.6 Efficiency of private sector ownership of toll roads: The M5 freeway in Sydney

The M5 freeway in Sydney, which takes traffic from the southern freeway, is designed to eventually become part of an orbital freeway network that takes traffic around the airport, through the city, under the harbor, and to the North. The freeway comprises M5 Central, which is privately owned and was built first; M5 West, which was funded largely by taxpayers in New South Wales and is now operating; and M5 East, which is yet to be built but could be either public or private. The owners of M5 Central have already benefited from the building of M5 West and will benefit even more once M5 East opens.

The auditor-general of New South Wales (1996) has pointed out that exits from the publicly funded M5 West cannot be completed because of the adverse consequences for the owners of M5 Central. He concludes that an urban toll road is not designed to efficiently meet the reasonable needs of the motorist but is designed to capture tolls and concludes that "private sector ownership of toll roads is prima facie less efficient than public ownership."

Opinions differ widely on toll roads. Private toll roads are considered most appropriate where restrictions need not be put on alternative traffic flows and where there is less network risk to the private project that the government has to cover. These conditions tend to be met on toll roads connected to bridges and tunnels.

measures of work, budgets, and specific tasks. The New South Wales system holds out the prospect of having the private sector bear much of the risk of managing the condition of the roads.

An interesting test of government commitment to private sector involvement was the decision to build the Eastern Distributor, which connects the center of Sydney to the airport, as a private toll road. Construction of the Eastern Distributor involves tunneling under the city, which means that it is relatively easy to build toll booths without disrupting traffic flows. The project sponsors have agreed to make improvements to the roads connecting to the city tunnel, which will improve toll revenue and traffic flow through the city to the airport and through the Sydney Harbour Tunnel, which the government effectively owns.

The government is attracted to the idea of a private toll road because only private funding would allow the project to be built before the 2000 Olympics, and the cost of constructing the road would have absorbed about 31 percent of the state's capital and maintenance budget for roads, a heavy burden to finance (box 2.7).

The main private rail project under way is the New Southern Railway, which will link Sydney's extensive rail system to the airport in time for the 2000 Olympics. This will be a BOT project, but the state will still own the track. The private consortium will own the stations. Most of the users will not be from the airport, but the airport traffic will pay a premium and will make the project economic. The siting of the stations was designed to improve the value of government-owned land. Preliminary scrutiny by the auditor-general suggests that this project may be less disadvantageous to the government than earlier ones.

Providing federal incentives for financing private infrastructure projects. The federal government did more to encourage private infrastructure

Box 2.7 Getting a better deal: The Eastern Distributor to the airport

In August 1996 the government of New South Wales announced that the Eastern Distributor linking Sydney to the airport would be built as a private toll road. The deal appears to be better structured than earlier toll road projects and pays more attention to network consequences.

Features of Eastern Distributor project

Feature	Contrast with previous projects
Government does not contribute to land or ancillary works.	• Government contributed A\$225 million to land acquisition and associated works for the M2 motorway.
• The Road Transport Authority (RTA) will be repaid for land acquisition costs.	
• Southern Cross Drive will be widened to six lanes and General Holmes Drive to eight lanes at no cost to the government; wider roads will be available to all road users, who need not use the northbound toll road.	• RTA purchased land for M5 motorway; cost was converted into a land acquisition loan to be repaid by the owners of the M5.
• Contractor will accept full risk of construction and traffic usage.	• Traffic usage of Harbour Tunnel is underwritten by the government, which provides a guaranteed revenue stream.
Improvements to public transportation are not limited by the deal.	
• Toll free access is available for government-owned buses providing public transport.	
• Development of other road or public transportation options is not constrained by the project.	
• Preferred proposal acknowledges that Eastern Distributor will be part of the principal north-south road corridor in this vicinity.	
• No renegotiation will take place if alternative public transport options are developed.	• M2 contract calls for renegotiation.
• Bus services for local residents will be improved.	
Urban amenities will be improved by tunnel.	
• Six-lane tunnel from Moore Park to north of William Street will reduce noise and visual impacts, removal of through traffic from streets will improve environment and amenity for local residents, and pedestrian black spot at Taylor Square will be eliminated.	
Toll will be collected in one direction only, and improvements will be made to toll-free routes.	• Tolls are collected in both directions on the M2 and M5 motorways.

Source: Australia, Ministry of Roads data.

than simply cut back on the ability of the states to borrow and cut their revenue grants. It introduced a range of incentives designed to overcome aspects of the Taxation Act that made it difficult to finance private projects. Infrastructure bonds were introduced and development allowances were provided for select projects. The federal government also took steps to compensate state governments that sold state enterprises that had previously been exempt from federal income tax but that lost their exemption when they were sold to the private sector.

The problem caused by the inability of a private project to offset the losses created in the early years against other forms of income for taxation purposes is a serious one. Australia has strict rules governing the transferability of losses between companies, which has meant that losses from a stand-alone project can be set only against future income and not against current income in an associated company. Since large infrastructure projects tend to incur losses in the early years and large profits in the out years, not being able to offset losses when they occur has made financing private infrastructure projects more difficult and expensive.

Generalized transferability of tax losses would have been very expensive, however. Instead, the government allowed approved projects to issue infrastructure bonds. The interest paid on these bonds is nontaxable, which makes them attractive to tax-paying bodies and allows the bonds to pay a significantly lower rate than they otherwise would. To prevent infrastructure bonds from becoming a general subsidy, the government does not allow a project to deduct the interest payments as a business cost, as would normally be the case. This means that infrastructure bonds provide considerable assistance to a project in the early years, when it is making losses, and offsets this assistance in the later years, when the project is making profits and cannot deduct interest as an expense. The net benefit to the project in present value terms is positive. Infrastructure bonds have been widely used in the financing of toll roads.

Learning lessons from experience. As their experience has grown, Australian state governments have developed clearer ideas about what role the private sector can and should play in the provision of infrastructure. Where these ideas have developed most clearly, so, too, has the commitment to put them into effect.

There is now wide acceptance that the private sector can proved several important benefits in the provision of infrastructure:

- It can generate investment that would be delayed if funded publicly—or not provided at all. This can have immense benefits if inadequate power, water, roads, and sewerage are constraining growth. Private funding of infrastructure can free up government resources for high priority social programs, such as public health and education, which could never be financed privately.
- It can produce large efficiency gains if a private plant is introduced into a public industry that has not previously operated on commercial lines and that has poor staff relations.
- It can help a public utility set prices that better reflect costs. Reaction to an increase in tariffs is often more muted if the utility is privately owned.

There is recognition that governments must know exactly what they are trying to achieve by involving the private sector and that they must exercise discipline in achieving their goals. This has not always been the case in Australia, where

some contracts were poorly structured. However, as governments have developed a clearer idea of what role the private sector should play, their capacity to negotiate tighter and better contracts has increased. Consultants to government have also played a pivotal role in building frameworks and overseeing negotiations.

Recognizing the different interests of different government agencies

Many different government agencies, each with different interests, are involved in infrastructure projects. Recognizing these interests and establishing clear-cut procedures for implementing projects is critical. Both public utilities and private sponsors must deal with a multitude of government agencies. But the public utility is treated as an insider and is often an effective operator within the government. In contrast, a private sponsor is usually treated as an outsider and lacks allies within the government.

The finance department

The finance department seeks to minimize public liabilities. If public funds are to be used, the finance department will want as little debt as possible raised and it will want to see a revenue stream to repay the debt. If the project is to be funded by the private sector, the finance department will not want the government to be drawn into government funding through guarantees to the project sponsors.

In Australia, as private infrastructure projects have been subjected to greater scrutiny, state treasurers have begun to require that interest rate margins properly reflect any government guarantees or commitments. This reflects both the growing sophistication of financial markets, which have tended to see through disguised financing arrangements and attribute liabilities back to the government when the public sector is in fact carrying all the risk, and heightened public sensitivity about tolls and contract details.

The industry department

The industry department seeks to maximize opportunities for local industry, whether the project is publicly or privately funded. It will expect a substantial proportion of the equipment used in the project to be manufactured locally and will want to see technology transfer and a commitment to export. Although the industry department may be supportive of private projects, private sponsors may find it difficult to comply with all the industry requirements, particularly if the department requires a high level of offset business.

The employment department

The employment department seeks to maximize opportunities for local employment. If skilled personnel are required, it will expect them to be trained locally, not brought in from overseas. Most private sponsors can make their projects attractive to the employment ministry by offering to train local residents to assume important positions created by the new project. One of the unexpected benefits in Australia of replacing state-owned enterprises with private firms has been the opening up of new career opportunities.

The environmental agencies

The environmental agencies will want to minimize the detrimental impact of projects on the environment. Given the long life of most infrastructure projects, most investors are interested in minimizing the risk of having to make expensive upgrades to environmental standards partway through the life of a plant.

The environmental agency can perform a helpful role by ensuring that proposed projects meet environmental requirements. The agency can cause confusion if it is not clear at which level (state, national, or international) responsibility for the environment lies, however.

The land acquisition department

Land acquisition can be difficult, particularly if it is left to the private sponsors to purchase required parcels of land. The nineteen toll road projects currently out for private tender in Indonesia require that the private contractor be responsible for land acquisition. Whether this requirement hampers the projects remains to be seen.

Many projects cannot proceed unless the government provides the land or is willing to use its powers for compulsory acquisition. But the department responsible for compulsory land acquisition will be reluctant to use its power to assist a private project.

The public utility

The public utility will try to maintain its central role. If the regulatory function has traditionally resided with the utility or been heavily influenced by it, the utility will resist change, even if its resistance endangers new private investment. In many cases the public utility will be the most difficult institution or agency to deal with, particularly if the utility believes that the private sector is being involved as a disguised financing vehicle to get a project built. If the government also believes the project is a disguised financing scheme, problems will inevitably arise, unless the private sponsors of the project accept the role the government assigns them.

Public utilities become concerned when change is proposed, and these concerns can make change difficult. For example, if contractual relations are to exist between the public utility and the private project, the public utility will want to maintain maximum control, even if such control raises the level of risk to the private project. The utility will often have powerful allies in this quest to retain control. It will suit the finance department, for example, to have all guarantees provided by the utility rather than the government. Retention of such control by the utility can weaken the private project if the financial standing of the utility is unclear, however.

The workforce of the utility will also feel threatened if it suspects that the private project is designed to benchmark more efficient levels of staffing. Workers and management of the public utility can be a powerful political force, particularly if the utility has a large investment program. In Australia in the 1980s, for example, the head of the government-owned telecommunications company often warned cabinet ministers of the impact that a cutback in the agencies' borrowing program would have on phone connections and investment in marginal seats held by the government in Parliament.

Federal-state issues

In a federation each state or provincial government will want to bring investment and employment to its region and will be distrustful of national guidelines. State and provincial governments will use their ability to withhold planning approvals to leverage their interests. Without coordination there is likely to be duplication of approvals processes. If a project can be sited in any of a number of states, the project sponsor can use the resulting competition among states to negotiate a better deal. State charges and taxes can be bid away in this process, and duplication of approval processes diminished.

Federal-state relations can often be perplexing to private sponsors, who may be unsure about who has final authority and what the real issues are. Matters can become very confused when one level of government assesses a project differently from another and takes policy action accordingly. This happened recently in Australia when the previous federal government disallowed private toll roads from qualifying for infrastructure bonds. The new federal government restored their eligibility.

Public utilities in East Asia are important bodies overseeing large and expanding investment programs. In 1993 an estimated $70 billion was spent on investment in the region, most of it publicly funded. This is quite different from the situation in South America, where the public utilities performed poorly before the recent round of privatizations. In many of the more successful East Asian economies the public utilities and authorities are functioning with some credibility. Cooperation between the officials responsible for key public utilities and the sponsors of private infrastructure is therefore essential.

Many public utilities and officials would like to take advantage of the expanding revenue resulting from economic growth and to implement commercial pricing on their own. If policymakers are not going to fund public investment, they need to make this clear to the public utilities by introducing a policy framework that defines the role of the private sector. Without clear policy articulation there will be ongoing confusion and resistance to change.

Negotiations over take-or-pay or power contracts should not be taken over entirely by public utilities. The minister needs a team around him or her whose experience is broader than that of the utility. While the government's negotiating team needs to understand the utility's interests, it also needs to be able to put those interest into a broader context.

Resolving issues

Handling the competing pressures of private infrastructure projects requires that ministers be committed to private sector participation and put in place administrative arrangements that allow competing issues to be resolved.

Coordinating government

Private infrastructure projects will stall unless the government establishes organizational structures to prevent government processes from overwhelming projects. Most countries try to deal with the complexity of the negotiations and the large number of government agencies involved by establishing central coordinating agencies. In Malaysia the coordinating agency is the Privatization Unit of the Economic Planning Unit in the Prime Minister's Office; in Australia the agency is the Office of Asset Sales in Canberra; in Indonesia the state secretary coordinates the processes. The coordinating agency in Malaysia is particularly powerful, since it comprises the Technical Committee and the Financial Committee, which evaluate and negotiate with the private firms (Yaacob and Naidu in this volume).

A properly functioning central agency can be useful if it brings all the agencies together and ensures that issues are resolved; if the central agency is just another layer of authority without the ability to deliver decisions from other agencies, it will only add to frustration. An all-powerful central agency can lead to another range of problems if it runs roughshod over other agencies without resolving legitimate concerns. If this is done, negotiations can be reopened only at great cost to all parties.

The process will be most efficient if over time an agreed upon framework can evolve that enables the following key issues to be addressed:

- The relationship between the private facility and the public utility and distribution system.
- The tax treatment afforded private projects. While individual tax rulings may be necessary, each project should not have to negotiate its tax treatment separately. If taxation arrangements are creating problems, they should be resolved for all infrastructure projects.
- Arrangements for supporting local industry, which should be understood at the outset and left intact as the tender process proceeds. If local industry preference is part of the tender process, it should be transparent.
- Requirements for training, environment clearances, and immigration, which should be understood at the outset.
- Authority over and responsibility for the project, particularly if there is significant opposition from certain agencies.

If senior ministers are firm, rules can impose structure and prevent particular agencies from constantly reopening matters and trying to reverse earlier decisions. Establishing a rule that tenders should be evaluated on the basis of world pricing of inputs would simplify dealings with the industry department, for example. If local industry preference is to be built into the process, a fixed level of preference (say, 10 percent) can be prescribed. Formalizing this process is preferable to having to make decisions about every potential domestic input. For rules to be effective, however, senior ministers have to be able to make decisions on the rules, and the rules have to be accepted as fixed.

Even when rules are established, however, issues will arise that cannot be determined on the basis of fixed rules. Some of these issues may be contentious. But decisionmaking will be simplified by establishing rules in advance and leaving commercial judgments to the project sponsors. Ideally, the sector or regulatory framework that the government devises to oversee the industry will answer most of the questions; as time goes on, the process may require less and less scrutiny. After the initial investment in the detailed framework, the government may well find that the process of selecting private infrastructure projects becomes more and more straightforward.

Both the private sponsors and the government need to accept a measure of self-discipline; both sides should avoid springing unexpected new demands on each other once either party is locked into the project. The temptation for either party to engage in "sequential ambush" is real, but the long-run consequences heavily outweigh any gains that might be extracted in the short run. The government must recognize that it will be seeking new private infrastructure repeatedly and that a reputation for springing new demands on project sponsors or changing the rules when it is very expensive to disengage will add to financing costs in the future, as sponsors try to protect themselves against the potentially higher cost of doing business. The private sponsor must recognize that a reputation for backing out of commitments at the last minute, failing to deliver on promises, or making new demands will make it very difficult to secure new business in the region. The last minute demand for government guarantees to cover construction risk in the Sydney Harbour tunnel project was difficult for the government to handle since by then it had no way of withdrawing from the project. Governments can protect themselves by not committing themselves publicly to a project until they have reached agreement with the main project sponsors on key issues.

Resolving federal-state disputes

In some countries, particularly those with strong state or provincial governments, uncoordinated and possibly confrontational relationships between policymakers at various levels of government may cause problems. When state administrations are strong, the central government may feel that it is losing its ability to control the macroeconomy if many major infrastructure projects remain outside its control. To regain control, the central authority will often announce guidelines governing projects. In many cases this may make sense, since it is efficient to have power, water, and transportation conform to national guidelines rather than uncoordinated state ones. (The Australian experience with six noncompatible state rail systems is a case in point.) However, central guidelines can cause problems if the coordination of state and federal guidelines has not been thought through.

In countries such as China, where the relationship between the center and the provinces is still evolving, private sponsors of infrastructure projects often find themselves entangled in complex and overlapping administrative arrangements. Individual states and cities can have considerable power to raise revenue and fund particular projects, but the central authority usually has sufficient power over taxation or exchange control to exert its authority if it wishes to do so.

Some promoters of private infrastructure have tried to minimize the difficulties that can occur by establishing direct commercial links with cities and states (box 2.8). While such a strategy may work for certain projects, particularly those that are commercial and not dependent on multilateral or aid agencies, it can add another element of risk to the project if the sponsor does not fully understand the relationship with the center. Without central government involvement and support there is also greater risk associated with enforcing contract provisions.

Regardless of a project's ability to deal directly with a city or state, there may well be a need for the central authorities to control behavior at the state level, especially when it comes to land acquisition and the provision of state services to the project. The central authorities may have to use their taxation powers and controls on borrowing and foreign exchange to prevent the project from being held hostage at the state level.

In Australia experience has shown that in a federal system in which the states have considerable power, heavy-handedness is counterproductive. The federal government needs clear instruments it can use to enforce its policies, but at the end of the day there has to be a measure of cooperation. In Australia this cooperation has come from regular formal high-level meetings between state and federal leaders, who have managed to agree on a range of national priorities they are willing to support. The Council of Australian governments, a body set up to deal with federal-state issues of national importance, meets regularly.

With national agreement has come a willingness to coordinate responses to infrastructure projects, particularly on environmental issues, where effort has been made to avoid duplicating environmental impact studies. Federal programs that provide for taxation incentives, such as infrastructure bonds and investment allowances for eligible infrastructure projects, have also encouraged the states to coordinate their processes with federal processes in order to make infrastructure projects eligible for federal incentives. As with most federal systems, there is scope for national coordination, but it is normally the federal government that has to pay to achieve it.

If there is a lesson to be drawn from the Australian experience with federal-state issues, it is that the federal taxation power is very important in building national responses. This lesson may have some relevance for countries such as China, where national-provincial relations are still evolving. The fact that Beijing is building a national taxation base to replace the income it received from public enterprises will change the relationship between the center and the provinces and may result in a steady increase in Beijing's authority over the provinces.

Obtaining the best deal

East Asian countries face tremendous opportunities for harnessing the private sector. Private sector investment in infrastructure can remove bottlenecks, improve economic growth, and reduce the social problems brought on by inadequate water, sewerage, transportation, and power. The private sector is keen to invest and will accept narrow margins if private firms are forced to compete. To negotiate effectively with private firms, however, government agencies may need to acquire new skills. Multilateral bodies and multicountry forums can help.

Scrutinizing projects

The potential gains from shrewd contract negotiation are enormous in twenty- to thirty-year take-or-pay contracts. These contracts are complex, legally dense documents the main purpose of which is to provide sufficient security to an

Box 2.8 Forging links with cities: The China Water Company

The China Water Company is a recently formed developer and investor in water supply, wastewater treatment, and water-related infrastructure in China established by AIDC Ltd., an Australian institutional investor. AIDC's equity holders are neither suppliers nor operators in the water industry but long-term investors from Hong Kong (China) and institutional investors of the Australian and Singapore governments. The company has initial shareholder funds of $30 million, shared equally between AIDC, Hong Kong Land, and Hong Lim Investments, a subsidiary of the investment holding company of the Singapore government. Chinese cities appear to see an advantage in dealing with long-term investors rather than with operators or suppliers who are seen as often being more concerned with short-run returns.

AIDC is building a commercial business with individual Chinese cities and does not deal with concessional lending institutions or multilateral bodies. The company uses appropriate local technology where possible and buys its water expertise on the market. It has entered into a joint venture with the Shenyang Water Supply General Company, a government-owned water utility company in Shenyang city, the capital of Liaoning province. The $25 million joint venture involves the construction, operation, and management of water facilities over a specified contract period. The project is expected to be completed within eighteen months and will supply 150,000 cubic meters of water a day to the local population. The company has also identified a number of other potential projects.

Chinese cities cannot borrow, but their authorities can, although they usually do not have the standing to do so. The China Water Company identifies an income stream; negotiates a contract with the water authority and the city, possibly involving a subsidy from the city; satisfies itself of the security of the arrangements; and builds the facility.

AIDC has found that avoiding aid agencies and multilateral lending institutions has made decisionmaking easier, and it has found the Chinese legal structure better than expected. The company has scope to expand, as many Chinese cities now have the income and wealth to finance water infrastructure on a commercial basis. It is estimated that to alleviate shortages China will need to build more than 230 new water plants similar in size to the Shenyang project over the next five years. Beijing's restriction that the private sector cannot own the water distribution system means that China's cities will be keen to use private capital to fund water treatment facilities to free up resources to improve distribution.

income flow so that financiers will lend to the project. Both the governments and the project sponsor and financiers will have expert advisers review the contract. These advisers will be very busy during negotiations (although the fact that their compensation depends on the amount of time spent suggests that in some cases negotiations may be prolonged unnecessarily).

While governments need advice on the complexity of the contracts, they also need the expertise to evaluate the broader ramifications of the project. With toll roads consideration has to be given to how competitive forms of transportation will interact. Future public investment in the network, which will affect the revenue of the toll road, also needs to be reflected in the negotiations. A new private water treatment plant needs to be coordinated with future public investment in distribution. A new private power generator requires investment in high-voltage and low-voltage distribution facilities to make best use of the private project. Future investment by the public sector made necessary by a private project should be reflected in the negotiations with the private sponsors, particularly if the private equity holders will benefit from future public

investment. For example, a private toll road may be very bankable because of its ability to raise a large revenue stream from motorists. But if it is connecting two toll-free public freeways, legitimate questions can be raised as to whether the project is earning an income stream from the new investment or from the existing investment in the two public freeways. In such situations closer analysis might suggest that the public sector join the two freeways. Even if the private project represents a disguised financing arrangement and the public sector benefits from commercial windfalls, all the costs to the public sector associated with the private project should be considered.

Governments sometimes feel more comfortable dealing with a businessperson or company with whom they have dealt in the past. Negotiations with such a person or company can often be more straightforward and speedy since there is a greater measure of trust and mutual understanding between the parties. Because they are perceived to have a lower level of political risk, such projects can sometimes be financed relatively more simply. In the long run, however, governments are likely to obtain better terms if they develop a framework within which a wide range of companies can bid on an arm's-length basis.

Governments are at a disadvantage when a private promoter devises a project and then proceeds to market it to the authorities, since the government is forced to depend on the expertise of the promoter to evaluate the project. Where proposed projects have been announced by the government and have not been subject to competitive tendering—as in the Sydney Harbour Tunnel project—or crucial financial issues have been developed in a post-tender arrangement, the government faces increased risks. Despite these drawbacks the Malaysian authorities have deliberately avoided competitive tendering. The government selects private companies with which it negotiates, and the private sector is encouraged to propose particular projects for privatization. Contracts in Malaysia have never been regarded as immutable, however, and the government can renegotiate aspects that are unsatisfactory (Yaacob and Naidu in this volume).

Reviewing projects: The role of the auditor

In Australia formalized review of the government's contracts with the private sector has been left largely to the State Auditor-General's Office, which audits projects and makes the findings known to state parliaments. State auditors-general are statutory officeholders, and although they are appointed by executive government their authority comes from Parliament. It is from the auditors-general in New South Wales and Victoria that the public knows so much about the Sydney Harbour Tunnel, the tollways, the water treatment works, and the costs involved in the sale of Loy Yang B.

Partly as a result of the work of the state auditor-general, the current government in New South Wales announced a formal policy entitled "Guidelines on Private Sector Participation in Infrastructure Provision." The guidelines cover the calling of tenders and the methods of selecting proposals.

The auditor-general does not have the power to scrutinize all documents, particularly documents held by the private sector, many of which are commercially sensitive. The extent of the auditor-general's powers over private infrastructure is still being debated in Australia, and some balance will need to be struck between protecting commercially sensitive documents of private companies and taxpayers' right to know what is being done in their name.

Establishing a regulatory authority

What happens if performance turns out to be radically different from what the financial modeling suggested? If the project generates more revenue than expected—because of greater productivity or lower costs—there will be political pressure to recoup some of the windfall gains for consumers. If rates of return are lower than expected, the project owners will want to revisit the pricing arrangements, something that governments usually resist.

In industrial economies governments establish independent regulators to deal with such situations. This would be done either by reviewing rates of return or by reviewing $CPI - X$ formulas at periodic intervals to keep a balance between the interests of the consumers and the private investors.

As East Asian economies develop and the private sector plays a larger role in the provision of infrastructure, the need will grow to require the review of tariffs in order to avoid abuse of market power. Arbitrary government discretion to adjust tariffs after contracts have been signed would make private infrastructure projects more difficult to finance on a project finance basis. Establishing a review process with accepted guidelines and methods of operation could reduce uncertainty and facilitate new private investment. In many jurisdictions the authorities retain the right to reopen contracts that prove to have undesirable consequences. In Malaysia, for example, the authorities have made it clear that contracts are not immutable, and contracts have been renegotiated. Such a system works in Malaysia because there is close communication between the government and private investors and because investors have been allowed to earn attractive rates of return. In the power sector independent power producers earn rates of return of 18–19 percent, and concession contracts for road projects are designed

Box 2.9 Promoting competition and investment in gas with a third-party access code

As part of the drive to build a competitive national market for electricity and gas, state and federal leaders in Australia agreed in mid-1995 to create the Gas Reform Task Force. The task force has set about developing a national code for third-party access to all pipelines. It covers both transmission and distribution systems. Federal and state representatives, regulatory agencies, the gas industry, and major consumers have all been involved.

The code will determine an access reference tariff, which will be based on a fair rate of return on assets. This will require financial modeling and careful valuation of assets. Effort has been made to provide incentives for discounts and to avoid passing on costs if the pipeline is not fully utilized. The natural monopoly elements of the gas industry are to be structurally separated, and the reference tariff will be adjusted by a $CPI - X$ formula.

Provision is also made for review of the reference tariff every five years in order to allow questions of excess or inadequate profits to be addressed. Not all issues would be subject to review, however. Structural issues would be set in stone to give certainty to the project, but market variable issues, such as demand, would be reviewed. This provision also enables the $CPI - X$ formula to be reconsidered every five years.

The model strikes a reasonable balance between the need for certainty and the difficulties associated with locking up the reference price for at least twenty years. The code reduces risk and is welcomed by investors in the gas industry and new investors seeking to compete by building new pipelines. The code will increase competition, but it will not get in the way of the original negotiations that underpinned the financing of the pipeline, since it will apply only to third-party users after the foundation users and suppliers have signed contracts that make the pipeline viable.

to provide investors with a return of 14–15 percent. However, East Asian governments may find it attractive to formalize informal review processes as contracts take on greater weight and they seek to strike even more competitive deals with private investors.

In Australia the current negotiations over a third-party access code for national gas pipelines illustrate how regulatory arrangements that open up new markets and provide for a fair rate of return on assets and periodic review can reduce uncertainty, encourage competition, and make private investment more attractive (box 2.9).

The first private project can act as a catalyst to regulatory change. The sale of Loy Yang B broke the mold in Victoria, and although it did not fit into any competitive model, it did force the government to think through the implications of a lone private supplier in a vertically integrated, publicly owned electricity industry.

Commencement of the Paiton Power Generating Complex in Indonesia is likely to lead to similar pressures. Already other private electricity projects are progressing on the basis of the Paiton contract, saving money and effort by simplifying the negotiating process. The fact that Paiton debt is now rated and trading in New York as investment-grade paper represents a major step forward. As all parties gain experience, new regulatory arrangements will need to be put in place to bring greater certainty to both existing investors and new entrants while promoting competition and efficiency.

Victoria has had great success with a pricing model based on splitting off the generators from the distribution function and forcing the generators to compete on pricing in a central pool. Elements of such an approach could be usefully introduced elsewhere. Malaysia has taken steps in this direction by selling off a share in Tenaga Nasional, previously the monopoly supplier of electricity in Malaysia. Five independent power producers have been allowed to supply electricity to Tenaga, with a separate regulatory agency set up to ensure fair pricing, prevent anticompetitive behavior, check prudent investment, and ensure safety in the industry. As well as corporatizing the old monopoly supplier and making it more responsive to market forces, the changes have brought new entities into the system that over time will serve as benchmarks against which efficiency can be measured. Pressure will continue to build to make tariffs competitive. As the system evolves and the independent power producers become more significant, this pressure is likely to lead to further regulatory reform. Malaysia may be influenced by the windfall that Victoria gained from selling assets and decide that it, too, wants to reap some of the benefits that can come from continuing to deregulate its system and selling off generation and distribution assets.

Improving public sector technical and negotiating skills

Public servants often lack technical and negotiating skills. The auditor-general of New South Wales (1996) has highlighted the question of the capacity of the public sector to negotiate acceptable arrangements with the private sector:

> The public sector typically does not have the prospect of commercial failure that helps to motivate the private sector. And it has not trained its public service to develop and assess what are often conceptually difficult arrangements. Moreover, the government does not reward its senior officers in the same way to the same extent as does the private sector. It would thus be surprising if the government's senior executive had the necessary skills to negotiate a balanced deal with the private sector. And if senior executives in the government sector have these skills, they must be tempted to seek employment with the private sector which actually pays for these skills.

Contract negotiations are normally based on financial modeling, which attempts to determine the rate of return generated by particular tariff structures. The task for the government and project negotiating teams is to arrive at a rate of return and a tariff that look reasonable to both parties and are acceptable to the financiers.

The financial modeling used by the parties is central to the negotiations, and it is essential that the government be in a position to build its own model rather than use a noncustomized model or depend on the model prepared by the project sponsor. Having the capacity to build a financial model and assess models built by others requires skills that all governments should possess.

It is clear that the public sector in Australia has been learning from its mistakes and has been developing new skills. It is also clear, however, that to a large extent different infrastructure sectors have failed to learn from the mistakes of other sectors. More can be done so that experience gained in one area of government is quickly passed on to other areas and so that experience gained in one country in the region can be transferred to other countries. Advisers with a broad understanding of policy are essential to complement the lawyers and other advisers. Outside consultants to the Victorian government, including Troughton Swier and Associates and Credit Suisse First Boston, have been at the heart of electricity reform there. Advisers can be trained or hired, and advisers and officials could rotate among East Asian countries.

Recognizing the advantages of a framework

The Australian experience reveals that a framework that sets out how private infrastructure projects will operate strengthens the hand of public sector negotiators, particularly if the framework promotes competition among the private sector bidders. Understanding the operating environment reduces uncertainty, which will enable the government to negotiate narrower margins with private promoters. If the government structures its framework to promote competition, it can gain an additional advantage by forcing private sector sponsors and investors to bid against each other to further compress margins without exposing the government or the community to additional liabilities or costs.

There is currently no shortage of private equity willing to invest in infrastructure projects in East Asia. Large infrastructure funds interested in long-term investment are located in Hong Kong (China) and elsewhere, and U.S. utilities are keen to invest in East Asian infrastructure projects as a way of lifting their overall earnings rate, the domestic part of which is held down by regulation in the United States. International companies that supply equipment for infrastructure projects, particularly power projects, are also keen to become equity partners, and energy suppliers want to participate in exchange for long-term contracts. National utility companies, such as Electricité de France, are also keen to invest as part of a national strategy. All these companies recognize that East Asia is the fastest-growing area in the world, that growth prospects are poor in Europe and elsewhere, and that the margins on their tradi-

Table 2.1 Proceeds from the sale of the distribution businesses and generators in Victoria
(millions of Australian dollars)

	United Energy Limited	Solaris Power	Eastern Energy	Powercorp Australia	Citipower Limited	Yallourn	Hazelwood
Sale date	August 1995	October 1995	November 1995	November 1995	November 1995	March 1996	August 1996
Book value	944	490	971	1,204	693	1,537	700
Gross proceeds	1,553	950	2,080	2,150	1,575	2,428	2,350

Note: United Energy Limited, Solaris Power, Eastern Energy, Powercorp Australia, and Citipower Limited are distribution businesses. Yallourn and Hazelwood are power stations.
Source: Victoria, Treasury Department data.

tional businesses are low. All have come to the conclusion that infrastructure investment in East Asia is one way of pursuing their corporate goals and increasing earnings. These companies are also attracted to spreading their investments across countries to minimize risk so that the investment interest is not concentrated in particular countries but is spread across the region.

At the same time Asian capital markets are developing rapidly, and there is growing scope for countries to finance private projects domestically without recourse to foreign capital. A developing domestic capital market is very important because it enables long-term investment and savings to be channeled into private infrastructure and allows the projects to be financed in domestic currency, thereby removing exchange rate risk from what are essentially domestic investments. The rapid development of Australian capital markets since they were deregulated in the 1980s has been very important in helping to finance private infrastructure.

Given the strategic concerns motivating many potential investors, governments have scope to extract premiums. In Victoria the state government created a framework that provided for the separation of the generators from the distributors, but it also provided for the sale of the regionally based distribution businesses and the generators. The five distributors and two generators were sold sequentially during the twelve months before August 1996. The tendering process raised A$950 million–A$2.4 billion for each business, for a total of A$13.1 billion from the five distribution businesses and two generators (table 2.1). At the time of the tendering process, these assets had a book value of about A$6.5 billion.

The bidders were prepared to accept considerable commercial risk once they felt the policy structure was secure. The distribution busi-

nesses were sold without guarantees, with the understanding that the exclusivity of their franchise was not watertight and that franchise customers who could not choose their suppliers would be protected by a $CPI - X$ regime that would set maximum uniform retail tariffs. By 2001 all customers would be able to choose whom they purchased electricity from, and they would be able to choose from a list of independent retailers that would include retailers from other states. Choice would be phased in, with the largest consumers having the opportunity to choose first.

In reality, each distribution area was relatively secure, but the distributors would have to compete for their larger customers and could not treat their smaller customers too casually. What made the distribution businesses attractive to the bidders was the fact that despite the uncertainty, the new arrangements provided the opportunity to introduce new technology and to retain the gains that might come from productivity improvements and cost reductions. What was offered provided enough security and business opportunity to make the distribution business attractive assets. The generators were sold without guarantees, with only the prospect of selling electricity in a wholesale market in which generators in other states with excess capacity would compete.

A wider range of equity holders were involved in the various consortia, including U.S. and U.K. power utilities and Australian superannuation funds. One of the reasons such high prices were realized was that funds managers believed that the electricity industry in Victoria was an attractive place to invest. This was the turning point and underscores why the sale process was so different from the sale process for Loy Yang B. Loy Yang B needed government guarantees and took an extended period of intense negotiations. The five distributors and two generators were sold within twelve months without guarantees. The difference was the framework and the fact that the distributors had a wider range of commercial opportunities because they sold directly to customers, unlike Loy Yang B whose output was sold on a take-or-pay basis to the wholesale pool. The fact that a national electricity grid and a competitive market for electricity will be functioning within the next few years has also added new commercial opportunities (see box 2.10 for an example of a sale under a competitive and stable market framework). The net result of these sales was that the state budgetary position was transformed and the state gained new budgetary flexibility.

East Asian countries could conclude from this that they, too, could extract competitive prices from the private sector if they established frameworks that provide less than exclusive franchises but allow direct sales to customers and genuine commercial opportunities. In exchange the private sector would accept mechanisms to protect customers from unfair trading. There need be no government guarantees if in the process of establishing the framework, the financial position of the various public utilities could be adequately scrutinized. If assets were also sold, East Asian governments could also find their budgetary position improved, with greater scope to channel resources into high-priority areas.

Recognizing the role of multilateral financial institutions

Multilateral financial institutions have traditionally played an important role in the provision of infrastructure in East Asia, providing finance, soft loans, and technical assistance. Today the financing task has become so large that multilateral financial institutions can play no more than a small role in financing. They can, however, play an important role in strengthening government institutions and their officials by providing training and by funding expert advice. In this way, governments can deal more effectively with project sponsors to everyone's advantage.

Multilateral institutions can also assist some countries with the tendering process by provid-ing advice and, if asked, assisting in the selection process itself. This role might be helpful in countries that are not accustomed to managing large international tendering processes on an arm's-length basis. Participation by a multilateral lending institution might spread the flow of information and help bring the expectations of all parties into line.

The Asia-Pacific Economic Cooperation (APEC) Energy Working Group, which comprises the United States, Japan, Canada, Australia, and the developing economies of East Asia, has been active building regional cooperation on energy matters. APEC brings a useful perspective to such issues as trade liberalization, standards, and infrastructure. It provides the leaders of the United States, Japan, and China with the opportunity to develop a common sense of purpose in a region in which the three powers have much at stake in building a creative and practical relationship.

APEC energy ministers met in Sydney for the first time in August 1996, when they endorsed a work program that will strengthen regional cooperation by, among other things, facilitating the seconding of regulators and other trained personnel among member economies. APEC also has the potential to speed development of sectoral and regulatory frameworks for energy. Its main strength, however, is that it is the only vehicle through which a number of important multilateral issues, including environmental issues, standardization of energy equipment, and security of energy supply, can be hammered out.

Environmental issues in East Asia need to be addressed on a multilateral basis. Without agreement among nations, individual countries may feel free to water down environmental controls in a bid to gain a competitive advantage. With the environmental consequences of one country's standards likely to affect other countries, there needs to be a venue in which these issues can be resolved. There may, in fact, be the making of an agreement under which various countries would provide assistance with new cleaner technology and cleaner coal that would benefit all concerned. APEC has the potential to build the confidence and mutual understanding necessary to make such agreements possible.

Box 2.10 Fetching top dollar when a competitive and stable market framework is established: The sale of Hazelwood Power Station

Hazelwood Power Corporation operates an integrated brown coal mine and a 1,600-megawatt power station located in the La Trobe Valley. The corporation was sold August 4, 1996, for A$2.35 billion. It had a book value of about A$700 million, revenue of A$255 million in 1995–96, and earnings before interest, tax, and depreciation of A$115 million. Revenues were expected to decline over the next few years, pending the full operation of the national market for electricity.

The corporation was bought by the Hazelwood Power Partnership, a consortium comprising Britain's largest electricity producer, National Power (52 percent), U.S. power companies Destec (20 percent) and PacificCorp (19.9 percent), and the Commonwealth Bank and its funds arm (8 percent).

The high price paid astounded the market. Hazelwood is a thirty-year-old plant, which many observers believed would be uncompetitive and would have to close once Victoria's electricity market was deregulated. In fact, the old State Electricity Commission of Victoria was set to close Hazelwood. Hazelwood's main attraction is that it should be able to operate as a low-cost base load facility selling into New South Wales and South Australia once the national grid is established. However, it will face fierce competition from New South Wales and Victorian suppliers, who collectively have excess capacity.

The sale underlined that the market will pay a high premium for a commercial opportunity once a competitive and stable market framework is established. The high price was achieved despite the government's refusal to allow a major equity holder in the Yallourn power station, U.K.-based Powergen, and a member of one of the losing bidders to have a degree of influence over Hazelwood's management. Powergen withdrew from the consortium.

Source: Victoria, Treasury Department data; *Australian Financial Review,* August 5, 1996.

The question of the security of energy supply is at the heart of many investment decisions, and coordination of electricity generating specifications has the potential to save more than A$10 billion, according to APEC. The fact that countries such as Indonesia and Australia, with their large energy resources, belong to APEC provides scope for further progress on this issue.

Conclusion

Involving the private sector in the provision of infrastructure opens up a wide range of opportunities. With private sector funds governments can make essential infrastructure investments even if they have limited scope to borrow or raise revenue. But to attract private sector interest and ensure that the state gets good value out of the private sector, governments have to develop sophisticated processes and acquire sophisticated skills. Private investment in infrastructure forces governments to identify and formalize arrangements that previously could be left unspecified when the system was entirely publicly owned. Learning to develop new systems is not straightforward, and governments frequently make mistakes along the way. But governments learn from their mistakes.

The Australian experience is similar to that of many countries in East Asia. Initially, the stimulus for private involvement in infrastructure came from the need to invest despite tight budget constraints, and investments in transportation, water, and power projects were little more than disguised financing transactions designed to get around budget funding problems. This phase also saw drawn out negotiations and the cancellation of projects. Although the private projects expanded supply, there was a feeling that governments could have negotiated better deals.

In Australia transactions have been left largely in the hands of state governments. Progress has been fastest in those sectors in which governments have tried to carve out a legitimate role for the private sector. In the state of Victoria, for example, the breaking up and privatization of transmission, generation, and distribution assets has transformed that state's budget position and has created a much more competitive and responsive industry.

Transportation has experienced a less radical transformation, and doubts over the desirability of private toll roads remain. But states have improved their ability to extract competitive bids from the private sector. State auditors-general have brought public scrutiny to a number of projects, strengthening the hand of government and narrowing margins. States have improved their ability to work closely with a number of potential contractors and have developed techniques to extract better deals. The fact that equity holders in a number of listed toll roads have done well has encouraged a range of new institutional investors, which has further strengthened the hand of governments.

Private water projects have developed steadily, and they, too, have benefited from public scrutiny and the growing number of private infrastructure funds. It is likely that the private sector will provide an important share of new investment in water treatment in the future, although there currently appears to be little interest in selling concessions or exclusive franchises.

Officials are still digesting the full implications of the recent experience, although some measure of consensus has occurred. Many now recognize the benefits of setting up a competitive framework and forcing private investors to bid against one another. There also appears to be agreement that competition and private ownership in the power industry can free up budget resources and improve efficiency. Better deals can now be secured in transportation and water, although for many the main attraction of private investment remains budget flexibility.

Private infrastructure promotes efficiency because it allows private investors to design and organize investment to minimize ongoing costs. Private investors are less likely to overengineer plants or invest where risk is too high. Benefits on this score are likely to be particularly important where the design of the plant has a large bearing on the cost of ongoing operations and maintenance.

What implications for East Asia can be drawn from the Australian experience?

- An innovative and flexible domestic financial market is important. Most private infrastructure projects are domestic and need to be financed in domestic currencies. Only when institutional investors are attracted to projects can governments negotiate narrower margins from private sponsors. Expanding private infrastructure and a developing domestic capital market seem to go together.
- Private investor interest in infrastructure is high, and private sponsors of projects will accept considerable commercial risk in

exchange for commercial opportunity if they believe the policy framework is stable. Governments can reap large returns by developing a detailed framework that sets out clearly the role of the private sector.

- If governments achieve the right balance between security of return and commercial risk, private sponsors will accept competition without government guarantees.
- There is a role for regulatory oversight, which can encourage competition, reduce uncertainty, and encourage new investment. Regulatory oversight is particularly important in the power industry.
- Even if the major objective in involving the private sector in infrastructure is to increase budget flexibility, governments can still negotiate narrower margins by negotiating with several project sponsors and increasing public scrutiny of negotiated deals.

Note

Don Russell is global asset adviser at Sanford C. Bernstein, New York. He was formerly Australian ambassador to the United States and has held several senior civil service positions in the Australian government.

References

New South Wales, Auditor-General. 1994. "Road Transport Authority: Audit of Infrastructure Projects." New South Wales, Australia.
———. 1996. "Financing Infrastructure: Private Profits from Public Losses." Paper presented to the Public Accounts Committee, Parliament of New South Wales, July 31.
Victoria, Auditor-General. 1994. *Annual Report*. Victoria, Australia.
World Bank. 1995. "Infrastructure Development in East Asia and Pacific: Toward a New Public-Private Partnership." East Asia and Pacific, Office of the Vice President, Washington, D.C.

CHAPTER 3

Contracting for Private Provision of Infrastructure: The Malaysian Experience

Yahya Yaacob and G. Naidu

Until just over a decade ago the provision of infrastructure in Malaysia was almost entirely the public sector's responsibility. Infrastructure services were considered far too important to be left to the private sector. And the Malaysian government, like many others, presumed that the technology and economics of infrastructure precluded any substantial role for the private sector. Because of natural monopolies, economies of scale, and externalities in the production and distribution of infrastructure services, infrastructure was considered more suitable for public provision than for private.

In the mid-1980s the Malaysian government initiated a program of economic liberalization and deregulation that included a comprehensive privatization policy. The policy entailed downsizing the public sector while expanding opportunities for the private sector. In infrastructure the opportunities for private sector participation in areas previously the exclusive domain of the government have expanded considerably—not only through the sale of equity in state enterprises but also through privately financed development of new services and facilities.

A shift toward private provision of infrastructure

The privatization policy had its origins in the macroeconomic problems Malaysia faced in the early to mid-1980s. Many of these problems were, rightly or wrongly, attributed to the government's increasing involvement in the economy, largely in pursuit of the objectives of the New Economic Policy. This extensive intervention in the economy led to a huge increase in the size of the public sector relative to the economy: the public sector grew from about 29 percent of gross national product (GNP) in the 1970s to a peak of about 58 percent in 1981. Public enterprises proliferated.

With the large government presence in the economy, the public sector deficit grew, leading to a sharp increase in domestic and external borrowing. External debt more than quadrupled between 1980 and 1985. Compounding this, the international recession in the 1980s dampened Malaysia's export earnings. The looming economic crisis culminated in a negative growth rate in 1985, the first since independence in 1957. By the late 1970s it was already apparent that government revenues could not keep pace with the growing expenditures. It was these circumstances that prompted the government's policy changes.

The shift in strategy from public-sector-led growth to private-sector-financed development began in 1983, when the prime minister announced a national policy relating to the concept of "Malaysia Incorporated." This concept sees the country as a corporate entity in which the government provides the enabling environment—infrastructure, deregulation, liberalization, and macroeconomic management—and the private sector serves as the main engine of growth. This policy marked the beginning of Malaysia's ambitious program of privatization. The government set out its rationale for privatization in *Guidelines on Privatisation* (Malaysia 1985). Implementation of the policy is guided by the *Privatisation Masterplan*, adopted in 1991

(Malaysia 1991a). The government's commitment to expanding the private sector's role in the economy is reiterated explicitly in its *Second Outline Perspective Plan* (Malaysia 1991b). The *Seventh Malaysian Plan (1996–2000)* confirms that privatization will be an important means of achieving the government's development objectives (Malaysia 1996). Infrastructure is at the forefront of the privatization program.

Over the past decade the liberalization and privatization programs have dramatically changed the conditions under which infrastructure services are provided in Malaysia. Private sector provision of infrastructure is extensive, encompassing ports, roads, power and telecommunications services, urban infrastructure, water supply, sewerage, and even hydroelectric generation (appendix table A.1). The privatization of state infrastructure companies and the opening of many segments of the sector to private participation have resulted in an important change in the respective roles of the public and private sectors in infrastructure development.

This shift is clearly evident in the financing of infrastructure development. Until the Fourth Malaysia Plan (1981–85) investment in infrastructure in Malaysia was entirely financed by the public sector. That is no longer the case. The growth in private financing of infrastructure has been so dramatic since the mid-1980s that during 1996–2000, coinciding with the Seventh Malaysia Plan, the private sector is actually set to spearhead infrastructure development in the country. During the Plan period the private sector is expected to invest 68.3 billion ringgit (RM), three and a half times the RM 19.2 billion that the public sector plans to spend on infrastructure (table 3.1). Including the resources that the private sector is expected to spend on the power industry would further increase the share of private financing in infrastructure development during the Plan period.

Contracts for private provision of infrastructure

The liberalization of entry into infrastructure sectors has not meant free entry: private firms that want to develop or operate infrastructure in Malaysia need government sanction in the form of a contractual arrangement with the government. Contracting between the public and private sectors in Malaysia for infrastructure provision, operation, and maintenance has taken various forms, the main ones being leases and concession contracts (appendix table A.1).

Leasing

Leasing is commonly used in privatizing state infrastructure companies. Under a lease agreement a public authority or agency transfers a state enterprise's physical assets to a private firm for a specified period, and the private company is required to purchase outright any moveable assets of the state enterprise, such as vehicles. The private operator is allowed to recoup its lease payments—which usually take the form of an initial payment and annual payments—and operating costs through user fees for the infrastructure services it provides. Since ownership of the physical assets remains with the government, the private operator assumes only operational risks. At the expiration of the contract the physical assets revert to the government.

In Malaysia leasing has been used most often in privatizing ports. The facilities at Malaysia's premier terminal, Klang Port, have been leased to three port operating companies, and four other ports are also being run by private companies under leases. Under two other lease agreements the corporatized railway company is operating the country's rail services and Malaysian Airports Berhad is operating its airports.

Concessions

By far the largest number of contracts used in the privatization of infrastructure in Malaysia have taken the form of concession agreements. Concessions incorporate all the features of a lease contract, but from the outset the private company has the additional responsibility of financing the construction of the project. Thus, unlike leases, which apply to existing assets, concessions are used for the development and operation of new infrastructure. In a typical

Table 3.1 Public and private financing for infrastructure development in Malaysia, 1991–2000
(ringgit millions)

Sector	Sixth Malaysia Plan (1991–95)		Seventh Malaysia Plan (1996–2000) Public sector allocation	Private sector investment[a] (1996–2000)
	Public sector allocation	Public sector expenditure		
Transport	12,881.6	11,594.7	15,484.2	—
Roads[b]	8,451.0	7,572.6	9,838.8	17,505.0
Rail	1,802.6	1,735.4	3,370.0	10,600.0
Ports	434.0	410.9	486.8	4,241.7
Airports	1,833.0	1,780.6	1,266.0	5,956.0
Urban transport	361.0	95.2	522.6	—
Utilities	2,876.3	2,796.7	3,687.3	—
Water supply	2,749.5	2,671.9	3,575.3	2,571.7
Sewerage	126.8	124.8	112.0	1,759.4
Communications	76.1	71.0	58.6	—
Telecommunications and postal services	45.0	39.9	25.5	25,660.0
Meteorological services	31.1	31.1	33.1	—
Total	15,834.0	14,462.4	19,230.1	68,293.8

a. Privatized projects. b. Excludes local roads in regional development areas, some local authorities, and agricultural roads, which have been allocated RM 700 million.
Source: Malaysia 1996.

concession agreement the private firm undertakes to finance the construction of an infrastructure facility and to operate it for an agreed on period. Consequently, in a concession agreement the private provider in theory assumes both the operational and the investment risks.

The Malaysian government has used concession contracts for the construction and operation of sixteen major urban and interurban road schemes, build-operate-transfer (BOT) projects involving a total investment of more than RM 17 billion. Three light rail transit projects in the capital city of Kuala Lumpur are being developed under concession contracts as build-operate-own-transfer (BOOT) schemes. Concession contracts have also been used for the development of new ports in Malaysia, the Lumut Maritime Terminal, and the Pelabuhan Tanjung Pelepas.

A variation of the concession is the contractual arrangement under which the independent power producer projects in Malaysia have been developed. In most countries such projects have involved both a BOT or BOOT concession agreement between the government and the independent power producer and a power purchase agreement between the producer and the (often integrated) national energy corporation. In Malaysia, however, private power generation was brought about through the issuance of licenses by the Electricity Supply Department to the independent power producer firms and a

power purchase agreement between the firms and Tenaga Nasional Berhad, the integrated power utility. The reason for this arrangement was that, from the very beginning, the government did not want to bear any of the project risks. The power purchase agreements are therefore the substantive contractual instrument in the development of private power generation in Malaysia.

Other forms of contracting

Three other contractual arrangements deserve mention. The first is a contract between the government and a private provider that essentially combines a lease and a concession agreement, used in privatizations in which the private company both takes over existing assets and is required to develop new facilities. The new terminal at Klang Port, Klang Multi Terminal, is one example of such an arrangement. Another is the privatization agreement between the government and the private operator of Johor Port (Seaport Terminal Sdn. Berhad), which consists of a lease for operating the existing facilities and a concession agreement to build a new port, Pelabuhan Tanjung Pelepas.

Management contracts are another avenue for involving the private sector in infrastructure. Under a management contract the private contractor is responsible only for the operation and management of the government-owned facility. This type of contract is rarely used in Malaysia's infrastructure sector. The government has signed a few management contracts in the water sector and a management contract for Penang Bridge that obligates the private firm to invest RM 500 million in improvements and repairs.

In some infrastructure industries the government issues licenses to private firms to provide services formerly provided exclusively by a government department or state enterprise. Privatized ports, for instance, operate under a license issued by the government, as do Tenaga Nasional Berhad and Telekom Malaysia. These licenses are time-bound and range from twenty-one years for Tenaga Nasional Berhad and Telekom Malaysia to thirty for most of the privatized ports. Licenses issued to private companies to provide telecommunications services are not time-bound. Although licenses are not in a strict sense contracts, like leases and concessions they too cannot be had on demand. They also impose implicit contractual obligations on the licensees, and failure to fulfill those obligations can result in termination of the licenses.

Contracting procedures

The procedures used in contracting depend on who initiates the privatization proposal. In Malaysia a privatization project in infrastructure can be initiated by either the public or the private sector. The procedures for awarding contracts in these two cases are similar though not identical.

Projects initiated by the public sector

A privatization proposal initiated by the public sector can be implemented in one of two ways. The government can choose or nominate a private company to undertake the project. Or, if the government has already undertaken a privatization feasibility study, it can direct the Privatization Unit of the Economic Planning Unit to offer the project for direct negotiation with a selected private company or to call for a restricted tender. The choice of approach and of the private contractor (even in the case of a restricted tender) is made at the highest political level.

The substantive contracting procedure is the same regardless of how the private contractor is chosen:

- The private company (or companies in the case of a restricted tender) is required to undertake a detailed feasibility study at its own expense and to prepare a detailed proposal.
- Two committees established by the Privatization Unit, the Technical Committee and the Financial Committee, evaluate the detailed proposal and undertake negotiations with the private firm. The committees then prepare a joint recommendation and submit it to the Economic Planning Unit.
- The Economic Planning Unit submits the recommendation to the Cabinet, which either accepts or rejects it.
- If accepted in principle by the Cabinet, the privatization proposal goes through a round of detailed negotiations between the private company and the relevant ministry.
- Upon completion of the negotiations, the privatization proposal is again submitted for approval by the Cabinet, which even at this point may reject it.
- If the Cabinet accepts the draft agreement (a lease or concession), the ministry and the private company enter into a contract.

Projects initiated by the private sector

A unique aspect of Malaysia's privatization policy is that it allows—even encourages—the private sector to initiate or propose projects for privatization. In such cases the contracting process is initiated by the private firm's submission of an unsolicited proposal to the Economic Planning Unit. If the initial evaluation finds merit in the proposal, the unit gives the firm a letter of intent and the status of "preferred concessionaire." This process is tantamount to first come, first served, because it very nearly accords the company that submits a privatization proposal exclusive right to undertake the project. But the company must still prepare and submit a detailed project proposal, including a feasibility study, for evaluation by the Technical and Financial Committees. The project then goes through a process similar to that for a proposal initiated by the public sector.

Basic features of the contracting process

Regardless of how a privatization project is initiated, the contracting process will always include certain basic features.

Length of negotiations. The larger the project and the more technically complex it is, the longer it takes to negotiate the contract. Most negotiations for infrastructure privatization in Malaysia, however, are concluded within six months, and lease contracts take much less time to conclude than do concessions. (Economic Planning Unit officials are of the view that contracting through open, competitive bidding would take much longer than the sole-source negotiated or restricted tender processes now used in Malaysia.) Because of the experience gained by the evaluating agencies and, equally important, by the private sector bidders, contracting now is said to take only half as long as when the privatization program began.

Critical negotiating points. The most important negotiating points in contracting for infrastructure projects relate to technical specifications, length of contract period, level of user fees (tolls, port fees, power purchase price), service quality standards, and government support (support loans, traffic volume supplements for toll roads, external risk supplements, government assistance in land acquisition). At the beginning of the contracting process the distance between the government's position and the private firm's is usually quite large. It is during the negotiations between the private firm and the Technical and Financial Committees that compromises are made and agreement is reached. The initial differences on nearly all the vital parts of the contract are now beginning to narrow, largely because both the government (and its agencies) and the private sector have become familiar with the range of technical and financial elements.

Scope of contract. A typical contract begins with a section containing the provisions of the concession agreement. Other important articles set out the design details for the project, the construction schedule, the toll rates or other user fees, the schedule of fee increases, and any government support to be provided. The other articles in a typical concession or lease contract pertain to termination of the contract and dispute settlement mechanisms.

Evaluation and negotiating mechanism. The Technical and Financial Committees are the principal government bodies for evaluating privatization proposals and negotiating contracts in Malaysia. Their formation has centralized the evaluation process, facilitating the entire contracting process. The effectiveness of the committees depends on the expertise and skills of their members. The members of the Technical Committee are drawn from the ministries and government agencies where the expertise needed to evaluate a particular proposal is available. Thus for a road project the Technical Committee would include, besides officials from the Privatization Unit, officials from the Infrastructure Section of the Economic Planning Unit and engineers from the Public Works Department, the Highway Planning Unit of the Ministry of Works, the Malaysia Highway Authority, and the Department of the Environment. For an independent power producer proposal the committee would include officials from the Energy Section of the Economic Planning Unit and the Electricity Supply Department. In addition to representatives from the Privatization Unit, the Financial Committee's membership includes staff from the Treasury, the Accountant General's Office, and the Attorney General's Office.

The two committees are also authorized to begin the negotiating with the private sector. Over time this task has been eased as technical benchmarks are established on the basis of earlier projects and as the committees gain experience in assessing the technical and financial parameters in the private sector proposal. The committees do not have the final word in negotiations. Contracts are fine-tuned at the Cabinet level and even during final negotiations with the ministry.

Open bidding or negotiated contracting?

The description of the contracting procedures above should make it evident that contracting for infrastructure privatization projects in Malaysia does not occur through transparent and competitive bidding. In fact, in the infrastructure privatization over the past decade only one contract has been awarded through competitive bidding (a small independent power producer project in the state of Sabah). In nearly all other infrastructure privatization—whether through divestiture, leases, or concessions—contracting has been through a sole-source negotiated process. In a very few cases, where the project was identified by the government, contracts were awarded through a restricted tender offer. Examples include the Kuantan Port privatization and the East Coast Highway, for which three firms were invited to submit tenders.

In both sole-source negotiated contracting and restricted tender offers, the private company has generally been selected by the country's political leader and the basis of selection therefore cannot be discerned. Despite the frequent criticism that the award of contracts in the infrastructure sector has lacked transparency and the accusations of political favoritism, the Malaysian government has rarely deemed it necessary to explain or justify its choice of contracting mechanism or of the firm to which a contract has been awarded.

There are three possible explanations of why the government has avoided competitive bidding. The first is a belief that awarding contracts through open, competitive bidding involves higher transaction costs than negotiated contracting. A second possible explanation is a belief that open, competitive bidding for contracts may make it difficult to achieve the New Economic Policy objectives. A third possibility is that the government has avoided open, competitive bidding because it is time-consuming. Negotiated deals apparently can be completed in half the time required for a competitive bidding process.

Contracting and efficiency

It could be argued that because contracts for infrastructure projects in Malaysia have not been competitively awarded, some of the potential efficiency gains from privatization have

inevitably been sacrificed. Although this may well be true, Malaysia's approach to contracting includes features that should offset at least some of the potential efficiency losses.

Negotiating process

The negotiating mechanism, especially the Technical and Financial Committees and the Privatization Unit, appears to function in a way that ensures that private firms cannot dictate the terms of contracts. Both committees have the requisite skills and expertise to undertake effective and meaningful negotiations with private firms, and it is generally agreed that they give their best effort to obtain the best possible terms for the government and the public. That the bureaucracy is a formidable negotiator is confirmed by many of the private firms now involved in the infrastructure sector.

There are numerous examples of the bureaucracy's effectiveness in negotiations. In many cases toll rate proposals have been scaled down during negotiations and lease and concession periods have been shortened. The most recent example is the reduction in the sale price of electricity from the Bakun Dam concession.

One factor that favors the bureaucracy in its negotiations with private firms is its information advantage. Work by government research departments, submissions by other private companies for the same project, proposals for similar projects, and other sources of information produce a huge database that the government can use to assess and evaluate privatization proposals. There have been so many road privatization projects, for example, that government departments and agencies are sufficiently well informed to undertake effective negotiations on all substantive issues of a road privatization proposal.

In addition to the bureaucratic scrutiny, there are at least two other levels of review at which contracts can be modified to take into account efficiency considerations and consumer interests. The negotiations are subject to scrutiny at the highest political level of the Cabinet, and contracts undergo final negotiation at the ministry level. Both processes help ensure that projects are efficient.

Specification of evaluation criteria

For all infrastructure sectors open to private sector participation in Malaysia, basic technical and financial standards and design parameters have been specified. And regardless of which approach has been used to award a contract, these standards must be met by the private supplier. For roads, for example, privatization proposals must contain a set of technical parameters that meet the standards for design, construction technology, pavement design, and the like that are set by the Public Works Department and the Highway Authority. For the financial evaluation, proposals must provide project cost estimates, traffic and revenue projections, a financial analysis, and a financial plan. These technical and financial criteria provide some assurance that the projects approved are efficient.

Allocation of risks

In the early years of infrastructure privatization in Malaysia some of the commercial risks of projects were borne by the government. But many of these risks have since been shifted to the private operators. Similarly, forms of government support once provided to private operators are no longer as readily available.

The experience with road projects illustrates the shift of the burden to the private sector. To enhance the viability of road projects, the government in the past gave private operators assistance in the form of support loans, traffic volume guarantees, and external risk guarantees and bore the full cost of land acquisition. But since 1995 the government has begun to transfer more of the risks in road projects to the private sector, including the cost of land acquisition. (However, the government still gives advances or interest-free loans to concession companies to alleviate the burden of financing in the early years of the concession.) The transfer of the cost of land acquisition to the concession companies means that they must now be more precise in their design work, resulting in less waste in land intake and thus greater efficiency.

In the electricity sector too there are signs that efficiency is now a greater consideration.

The first independent power producer project was developed under a take-or-pay power purchase agreement providing little incentive for efficiency. For the next four such projects the agreement did not include take-or-pay provisions, so that the most efficient power producer would be the first allowed to supply the grid. Changes have also been made in the pricing mechanism to force power producers to increase efficiency. The independent power producer pass-through in the pricing formula was discontinued, and the automatic rate revision clauses have been removed from the licenses granted to privatized utility companies.

The role of consumers

Whatever the mechanism by which the contract was awarded, privatization projects have increasingly had to stand up to scrutiny by Malaysian consumers. On many occasions the public has expressed dissatisfaction over the levels of toll rates, telephone rates, electricity rates, and fees for sewerage services, forcing the government to renegotiate with the concessionaires.

Factors in the success of contracting in Malaysia

Even if contracting in Malaysia cannot be said to guarantee efficient infrastructure provision, there is no doubt that, unlike many other countries, Malaysia has succeeded in attracting significant private resources to its infrastructure sector. In addition to the projects already completed and under way, many proposals are under consideration for the privatization of existing ports, the development of new port terminals, the privatization of roads, and the development of independent power producer projects.

What explains the government's success in contracting with private firms for the supply of infrastructure services? There are three main factors. First, the government has a substantial and credible commitment to the privatization of infrastructure. Second, the government has consistently shown a genuine interest in making privatization projects succeed even if that means renegotiating with the private operators. And third, the straightforward institutional structure for infrastructure privatization and the harnessing of expertise and skills at the Economic Planning Unit to evaluate and negotiate project proposals have facilitated contracting.

There is strong commitment to the privatization policy among the country's political leadership. Prime Minister Mahathir's personal interest in the privatization program lends considerable credibility to the policy. The political stability and the overwhelming strength of the ruling coalition party also help assure the private sector that the privatization policy and the economic liberalization program will be sustained. The *Guidelines on Privatisation, Privatisation Masterplan,* and *Second Outline Perspective Plan* all confirm the government's commitment to privatization. The high-level commitment creates an environment conducive to contracting by limiting the government's ability to behave opportunistically.

The bureaucracy's attitude toward the private sector has become increasingly positive since the government's adoption of the Malaysia Incorporated concept. The public sector is now encouraged to view the private sector as a partner in development and to work to ensure the success of privatization projects. One outcome of this approach relates to the provision of information to private firms to assist their project preparation. Feasibility studies undertaken by the government or its agencies are now readily made available to the private firms selected to bid for a project, and departments are encouraged to support the firms' project preparation.

The public sector's commitment to making privatization projects succeed is reflected in the government's flexible approach to implementing contracts, best illustrated by projects that need to be renegotiated. Contracts have often been modified by mutual agreement because of unanticipated events—sometimes to protect government or consumer interests and sometimes at the request of the private firm. There have been at least four major renegotiations in recent years, and the expeditious settlement of the issues reflects both the government's commitment to projects' success and the private sector's belief that the government is renegotiating in good faith. The following examples illustrate

the flexible manner in which privatization contracts are implemented in the country:

- Public protests over the imposition of tolls by the private developer of an urban road project in Kuala Lumpur led the government to renegotiate the contract so as to reduce the tolls and delay their imposition.
- In the Kelang Container Terminal privatization agreement the lease contract gave the company exclusive rights to provide container handling services at Klang Port. Soon after the agreement was signed the government realized that granting these exclusive rights had been a grave error. When the remaining facilities at Klang Port were leased to a new port operating company that was also allowed to develop its own container berths, the government persuaded Kelang Container Terminal to drop its exclusive rights. In return the government allowed the company to expand its terminal from three container berths to four.
- At the beginning of 1996 PLUS, the concession company for the North-South Expressway, was entitled under the concession contract to raise its toll rates. But the government persuaded the company to delay the toll hikes and reduce the increase and began negotiating with PLUS the compensation for this change to the contract.
- As a result of much public dissatisfaction with the way the national sewerage project was being implemented under a concession contract with Indah Water Konsortium, the government commenced renegotiation of the contract.
- In 1994 the minister responsible for telecommunications issued a number of new licenses. In early 1996, however, the new minister of energy, telecommunications, and post thought that too many licenses had been issued and encouraged consolidation of the industry through mergers among the firms. The matter is now being left entirely to the private sector.

These examples suggest that contract renegotiations have been common in Malaysia. But they have been neither time-consuming nor costly. The government's flexibility has contributed to this. In addition, private infrastructure firms have been extremely cooperative, in part because they depend on the goodwill of the government for future projects. Renegotiation is also eased by the operational auditor system, in which one auditor comes from the government and the other from the private company. This system minimizes disputes over requests for renegotiation.

Also important in Malaysia's success in contracting out the provision of infrastructure to private firms is the simple institutional structure created to deal with infrastructure privatization. The Privatization Unit and the Technical and Financial Committees constitute an effective and inexpensive contracting mechanism, and the procedures for gaining approval for privatization projects are fairly straightforward. The Privatization Unit acts as a one-stop agency, although approval is also needed from the Cabinet and the relevant ministries. But the triple-layered approval system does not appear to be overly cumbersome or complex. Contract disputes are to be settled by arbitration in accordance with the arbitration rules of the United Nations Commission on International Trade Law. There is no provision for legal resolution of disputes.

Also contributing to the rapid pace of infrastructure privatization in Malaysia is the rate of return that the government allows private firms to earn from investments in the sector. Independent power producers typically earn returns of about 18–19 percent, and concession contracts for road projects are generally tailored to give investors a return of 14–15 percent.

Note

Yahya Yaacob is secretary general of the Ministry of Works, Malaysia, and G. Naidu is an associate professor at the University of Malaya.

References

Aida, Boey Abdullah. 1996. "Malaysia: Towards Vision 2020—The Privatization and Road Development Strategy." Economic Planning Unit, Prime Minister's Department, Kuala Lumpur.

Hitam, Samsudin bin. 1995. "Transport Infrastructure for Economic Development: The Case for Malaysia." Paper presented at the Asian Conference on Emerging Role of the State in the Transport Sec-

tor in the Perspective of Economic Liberalization, New Delhi. Economic Planning Unit, Prime Minister's Department, Kuala Lumpur.

Ibrahim, Abdul Khalid bin. 1987. "Privatisation and the New Economic Policy." Paper presented at the National Conference on Privatisation: Towards the Formulation of a Masterplan, Institute of Strategic and International Studies, Kuala Lumpur. Perbadanan Nasional Berhad, Kuala Lumpur.

Jomo, K.S., Christopher Adam, and William Cavendish. 1995. "Policy." In K.S. Jomo, ed., *Privatising Malaysia: Rents, Rhetoric, Realities.* Boulder, Colo.: Westview.

Kennedy, Laurel. 1995. "Telecommunications." In K.S. Jomo, ed., *Privatising Malaysia: Rents, Rhetoric, Realities.* Boulder, Colo.: Westview.

Lee, Cassey. 1995. "Regulatory Reform in the Infrastructure Sector: The Malaysian Experience." Paper presented at the Regional Workshop on Managing Regulatory Policies and Reforms in East Asia, World Bank and the Institute of Strategic and International Studies, Kuala Lumpur, July. University of Malaya, Kuala Lumpur.

Malaysia, Economic Planning Unit, Prime Minister's Department. 1985. *Guidelines on Privatisation.* Kuala Lumpur: National Printing Department.

———. 1988. "National Ports Plan." Vol. 1, "Overview." Prepared by PRC Engineering, Inc., in association with Sepakat Setia Perunding Sdn. Berhad and Aseambankers Malaysia Berhad, Kuala Lumpur.

———. 1991a. *Privatisation Masterplan.* Kuala Lumpur: National Printing Department.

———. 1991b. *The Second Outline Perspective Plan, 1991–2000.* Kuala Lumpur: National Printing Department.

———. 1996. *Seventh Malaysia Plan (1996-2000).* Kuala Lumpur: National Printing Department.

Malaysian Economic Association. 1991. "Bintulu Port Privatization Study." Vol. 1. Kuala Lumpur.

Naidu, G. 1992. "Private Provision of Physical Infrastructure: The Malaysian Experience." Economic Development Institute Working Paper. World Bank, Washington, D.C.

———. 1995. "Infrastructure." In K.S. Jomo, ed., *Privatising Malaysia: Rents, Rhetoric, Realities.* Boulder, Colo.: Westview.

Naidu, G., and Cassey Lee. 1997. "Malaysia: The Transition to Privatization." In Ashoka Mody, ed., *Infrastructure Strategies in East Asia: The Untold Story.* Washington, D.C.: Economic Development Institute, World Bank.

Ng, Chee Yuen, and Toh Kin Woon. 1992. "Privatization in the Asian-Pacific Region." *Asian Pacific Economic Literature* 6(2).

Puthucheary, Mavis. 1987. "An Assessment of the Privatization Guidelines with Reference to Objective Setting." Paper presented at the National Conference on Privatisation: Towards the Formulation of a Masterplan, Institute of Strategic and

International Studies, Kuala Lumpur. University of Malaya, Kuala Lumpur.

Salleh, Ismail Muhd. 1991. "Privatization: The Malaysian Experience." In Hisashi Yokoyama and Mokhtar Tamin, eds., *The Malaysian Economy in Transition.* Tokyo: Institute of Developing Economies.

Salleh, Ismail Muhd, and Saha Dhevan Meyanathan. 1993. *Malaysia: Growth, Equity, and Structural Transformation.* Lessons of East Asia Series. Washington, D.C.: World Bank.

Salleh, Ismail Muhd, and H. Osman-Rani. 1991. "The Growth of the Public Sector in Malaysia." Institute of Strategic and International Studies, Kuala Lumpur.

Shawal, Abdul Hamid. 1996. "Malaysia Privatization Experience—Past Success, Future Challenges, and an Update on the Malaysian Privatization Master Plan." Paper presented at the National Privatization Summit: Privatization—The Next Steps, Kuala Lumpur. Economic Planning Unit, Prime Minister's Department, Kuala Lumpur.

Sulaiman, Ali Abul Hassan bin. 1993. "Financing Infrastructure Projects: Issues and Recent Policy Developments." Paper presented at the Regional Conference on Financing Infrastructure Projects in South-East Asia, Kuala Lumpur. Economic Planning Unit, Prime Minister's Department, Kuala Lumpur.

———. 1994. "Infrastructure Development for Economic Growth: The Case of Malaysia." Paper presented at the World Infrastructure Forum, Jakarta. Economic Planning Unit, Prime Minister's Department, Kuala Lumpur.

Appendix
Table A.1 Infrastructure privatization and contracting in Malaysia

Sector and project	Method of privatization	Type of contract
Ports		
Klang Port		
Kelang Container Terminal	Sale of equity (1986)	Lease (21 + 30 years)
Kelang Port Management	Sale of equity (1992)	Lease (30 + 30 years)
Klang Multi Terminal	Sale of equity and BOT (1994)	Lease (30 years) and concession (33 years)
Johor Port	Sale of equity (1995)	Lease (30 + 30 years)
Bintulu Port	Corporatization (1993)	Lease
Penang Port	Corporatization (1994)	Lease
Lumut Maritime Terminal	BOOT (1993)	Concession
Pelabuhan Tanjung Pelepas	BOOT (1995)	Concession
Kuantan Port	Sale of equity[a]	Lease
Roads		
North Klang Straits Bypass	BOT (1984)	Concession (25 years)
Jln. Kuching/Kepong Interchange	BOT (1985)	Concession (16 years)
KL Interchange	BOT (1987)	Concession (30 years)
North-South Expressway	BOT (1988)	Concession (30 years)
Second Link to Singapore	BOT (1993)	Concession (30 years)
Penang Bridge	Management contract (1993)	Management contract (25 years)
Butterworth-Kulim Expressway	BOT (1994)	Concession (32 years)
Seremban–Port Dickson Highway	BOT (1994)	Concession (30 years)
Shah Alam Expressway	BOT (1994)	Concession (29 years)
North-South Expressway Central Link	BOT (1994)	Concession (25 years)
KL-Karak Highway	BOT (1994)	Concession (27 years)
New North Klang Straits Bypass	BOT (1995)	Concession (25 years)
Cheras-Kajang Highway	BOT (1995)	Concession (30 years)
Elevated Highway over Sg. Klang and Sg. Ampang	BOT (1996)	Concession (33 years)
Damansara-Puchong–Putra Jaya Highway	BOT (1996)	Concession (33 years)
New Pantai Highway	BOT (1996)	Concession (30 years)
Sungai Besi Road	BOT (1996)	Concession (30 years)
Water supply		
Labuan Water Supply	BOT (1987)	Concession
Ipoh Water Supply	BOT (1989)	Concession
Larut Matang Water Supply	BOT (1989)	Concession
Semenyih Dam	Management contract (1987)	Management contract
Tube well maintenance, Labuan	Management contract (1988)	Management contract
Johor Water Authority	Corporatization (1994)	Lease
Pulau Pinang Water Authority	Corporatization (1987)	Lease
Power		
Tenaga Nasional Berhad	Sale of equity (1992)	License (21 years)
Independent power producers		
YTL—Paka and Pasir Gudang	BOT (1995)[b]	Power purchase agreement (21 years)
SEV—Lumut	BOT (1996–97)[b]	Power purchase agreement (21 years)
GSP—Sepang	BOT (1994–96)[b]	Power purchase agreement (21 years)
PDP—Port Dickson	BOT (1995)[b]	Power purchase agreement (21 years)
PSP—Powertek, Malacca	BOT (1995)[b]	Power purchase agreement (21 years)
Telecommunications		
Telekom Malaysia Berhad	Sale of equity (1990)	License (21 years)
Ten private telecommunications operators		License
Others		
KTM Berhad (Malayan Railway)	Corporatization (1992)	Lease
Malaysian Airports Berhad	Corporatization (1992)	Lease
National sewerage system	BOT (1992)	Concession (28 years)
Light rail transit system I (phase 1)	BOOT (1993)	Concession (60 + 60 years)
Light rail transit system I (phase 2)	BOOT (1994)	Concession (60 + 60 years)
Light rail transit system II	BOOT (1994)	Concession (60 + 60 years)

Note: BOT is build-operate-transfer; BOOT is build-operate-own-transfer.
a. Transaction was pending in 1996.
b. Date of commissioning.
Source: Naidu 1995 (updated by author).

CHAPTER 4

Regulating Private Involvement in Infrastructure: The Chilean Experience

Alejandro Jadresic

Expanding infrastructure is a main challenge for the Chilean economy. Rapid economic growth, which has averaged 7.4 percent annually over the past decade, is requiring massive investment in energy, telecommunications, roads, railroads, ports, airports, water supply, and irrigation. In the next six years the economy is expected to grow at about 6.0 percent annually and total investment requirements in infrastructure are estimated at more than $18 billion (table 4.1).

In order to meet such needs without endangering the budget and diverting resources from pressing social needs, Chile has implemented a policy that allows the private sector to take the lead in infrastructure investment. Private companies should meet almost all new investment requirements in telecommunications and energy and a major share in the remaining sectors. In the next six years private investment in infrastructure should account for about $13 billion, or more than 70 percent of required investment.

Private participation in infrastructure implies more than capital investment. Chilean policymakers also rely on the private sector to plan, build, and operate infrastructure, and to manage the commercial risks associated with infrastructure projects. The Chilean economy benefits not only from the financial resources provided by private investors but also from their managerial and technical skills.

Major reforms have been introduced in the Chilean economy in order to involve the private sector in infrastructure, and reforms are still taking place, since the government is committed to creating new opportunities for private initiative. Such reforms have significantly changed the structure and operations of the infrastructure sector.

From state to markets: A historic overview

Until the 1970s the state was the main player in Chilean infrastructure. Through government institutions and state-owned companies, it was the role of the state to plan, finance, build, and operate most of the country's infrastructure. Then in the late 1970s government reforms began to reverse the roles. Privatization of the power and transportation sectors is now nearly complete, and private investment is flowing into infrastructure construction.

Major state involvement

Before the Second World War the state was heavily involved in building roads, ports, railroads, airlines, irrigation works, and waterworks. After the war state involvement strengthened as a result of policies that explicitly promoted government intervention in developing basic infrastructure. State-owned companies were created for electricity, oil, telecommunications, shipping, and urban transportation. Private companies in such sectors were transferred to government ownership. State monopolies became the norm.

By the early 1970s it had become the government's responsibility to operate and develop new infrastructure, relying on the national budget or income earned by state-owned companies. The government set the prices charged to customers at levels that were insufficient for self-financing but that reduced inflationary pressures on the economy. Capital shortages became common in the infrastructure sector, and national investment plans could not be completed. Financial deficits worsened in state companies in which social objectives had fostered the hiring of excess personnel.

Customers had no choice but to accept conditions imposed by the sole state supplier. Protectionist policies had progressively been imposed, severely limiting any opportunity for new investors to enter the market. Barriers to entry also existed in such sectors as fuel distribution, air transportation, and shipping, where privately owned companies remained as important players.

The shift to private provision

In the late 1970s the government introduced radical reforms in the Chilean economy. The guiding principles of such reforms were to reduce the intervention of the state in the economy, promote private initiative, open markets to international trade and foreign investment, stimulate domestic competition, and lift restrictions limiting access of new actors in the infrastructure market. State-owned companies were required to finance their operations and investment plans out of earnings. Prices were deregulated when competition was feasible or set at levels that would cover costs when state monopolies were the service providers. State-owned companies were forced to reduce costs and to fire excess personnel. Stringent budgetary limits were imposed, constraining not only internal operations but also investment plans.

Once these new economic rules were in place and state-owned companies had balanced their budgets, the decision was made to privatize those activities that could be run on a commercial basis. The government realized that only the private sector could provide the funds required to resume investment in expansion of domestic infrastructure. In many cases privatization had to be preceded by legal reforms in order to transfer to the government regulatory and planning activities previously performed by state companies and to establish competitive regulatory

Table 4.1 Estimated infrastructure investment requirements in Chile, 1995–2000
(US$ millions)

Sector	Investment requirements
Highways	4,250
Urban roads	2,000
Water supply	950
Sanitation	1,480
Community facilities	810
Ports	450
Railroads	470
Irrigation	370
Subways	520
Airports	100
Rain water and river management	195
Power industry	3,000
Gas industry	1,500
Telecommunications	2,500
Total investment requirements	18,595

Source: Chile, Ministry of Public Works data.

frameworks. Administrative actions were taken to split up large enterprises or transform them into private corporations.

Starting in the late 1970s and continuing through the 1980s, many companies were privatized in the infrastructure sectors, including the gas distribution company, the telephone company (Compañía de Teléfonos de Chile, or CTC) and two other telecommunications companies, five power generation companies, eleven power distribution companies, and an airline (table 4.2). The story of privatization of the electricity and telecommunication sectors is told in case studies later in this chapter.

Different sale schemes were used in the privatization process. In the first phase, through 1985, entire companies were sold. This made for a faster sale to a single bidder. However, only a few investors could qualify as potential bidders, given the amounts of capital required; at this stage institutional and foreign investment was not yet important. As a consequence, property was concentrated in a few hands. It was also argued that the prices paid were too low.

To overcome these problems, the next phase of privatization considered a greater diffusion of property. Very often some shares were kept aside for purchase by employees or for civil servants with the help of long-term credit schemes. The state also granted soft loans to individuals to buy a limited number of shares, which was called popular capitalism. During this period controlling shares were auctioned only in the

Table 4.2 Infrastructure companies privatized in Chile, 1976–90

Company	Year[a]	Sector
Gasco	1977	Gas distribution
Frontel	1980	Power distribution
Saesa	1980	Power distribution
Chilmetro	1986	Power distribution
Emec	1986	Power distribution
Emel	1986	Power distribution
Pilmaiquén	1986	Power generation
Télex - Chile	1986	Telecommunications
Chilgener	1987	Power generation
Chilquinta	1987	Power distribution
CTC	1987	Telecommunications
Emelat	1987	Power distribution
Pullinque	1987	Power generation
Edelmag	1988	Power generation and distribution
Endesa	1988	Power generation
Entel	1988	Telecommunications
Elecda	1989	Power distribution
Eliqsa	1989	Power distribution
Emelari	1989	Power distribution
Lan Chile	1989	Air transport
Pehuenche	1989	Power generation

a. Refers to the year private capital gained control of the company.
Source: Sáez 1993.

Table 4.3 Infrastructure companies privatized in Chile in the 1990s

Company	Year[a]	Sector
Edelnor	1994	Power generation and transmission
Fepasa	1994	Railroads
Empremar	1995	Shipping
Colbún	1996	Power generation
Ferronor	1996	Railroads
Tocopilla	1996	Power generation

a. Refers to the year private capital gained control of the company.
Source: Based on private communication of Rosella Cominetti (Economic Commission for Latin America).

few cases where massive investment was required to boost company development.

Domestic pension funds played a crucial role in the privatization of state-owned companies, at a time when few large domestic or foreign investors were willing to invest in what was seen as a bold liberal experiment in a developing country with high political risks and unproven regulatory norms. The private pension fund system had been created in the early 1980s as a replacement for the almost bankrupt social security system. The new system introduced individual accounts managed by private companies in a competitive environment regulated by the state. Workers were required to deposit a set share of their earnings in these accounts, with benefits based on the accumulated value of the accounts at the time of retirement. Using these forced savings, the new pension funds acquired large shares in privatized companies, particularly in the power and telecommunications sectors. To this day they remain a major supplier of funds for the ambitious investment programs that these companies are undertaking in Chile and in neighboring countries.

During the 1990s privatization of the power sector was completed and that of the transportation sector was begun. Control of all power

companies has been transferred to the private sector, with special safeguards to ensure the entry of new players and greater competition. The state shipping company was sold during this period, and privatization of the railroad system was initiated in order to stimulate investment and modernization (table 4.3). Investment during the 1980s in the state-owned railroad had been very low, leading to infrastructure deterioration and a decline in railroad use. After a 1992 law allowed the railway company to create a partnership with the private sector, a controlling share of the rail freight business was privatized, forming two companies: Fepasa, covering the southern and central part of the country (1995), and Ferronor, covering the north (1996). In the passenger business, in both suburban and interurban services, conditions are being created to promote private sector participation. A system is being defined that will allow private companies to bid for a concession granting them the right to run passenger services on a commercial basis. In some cases in which the social rate of return is satisfactory but the commercial return is not, a one-time lump-sum subsidy may be considered.

A concessions law has been approved in order to promote private investment in roads, tunnels, and other transportation infrastructure. Concession arrangements allow major projects to be developed and financed by private consortia that recover their investments by charging user fees. This system is described in the road and transportation case study later in this chapter.

The next round of privatization will affect ports, water supply, and sanitation. For these sectors the government has proposed legal reforms allowing all new investment to come from the private sector. In the case of ports, state-owned regional companies will privatize operations. In the case of water supply, privatization of 65 percent of the shares of state-owned companies is being considered. Progress to date in delineating public and private roles in the water supply and sanitation sector is described in a case study later in this chapter.

Guiding principles

Private participation in Chilean infrastructure sectors is guided by four basic principles, embodied in existing laws and in government policies and initiatives: promote private investment, strengthen competition, protect the environment, and satisfy basic social needs. The balancing of these objectives requires a sound regulatory system.

Promoting private investment

Shortage of infrastructure can become a bottleneck for development, requiring allocation of massive resources to new projects. But funds are required to meet pressing investment needs in social areas such as education, health, and housing, where it is difficult to attract private capital. In fact, at present 70 percent of the state's budget is allocated to social areas. There is no choice but to rely on private capital for infrastructure expansion. In addition, private participation works as a mechanism to promote efficiency in constructing and operating infrastructure: the profit motive makes cost reduction a high priority.

Chile has been very successful in promoting private investment in infrastructure. A key incentive has been the persistence of a favorable investment climate in the economy as a whole. A stable political system, a well-developed financial sector, openness to trade and foreign investment, and capable government institutions have contributed to this climate. In addition, regulatory norms established for the main sectors have applied clear and stable rules. The duties and rights of private operators are defined in sectoral laws, which clearly distinguish the regulatory role of the state and the managerial role of both private and state-owned companies.

The positive business climate and existence of clear rules have been important not only for privatizing state-owned companies but also for maintaining the flow of investment. In fact, privatized Chilean infrastructure companies have become major investors in other sectors in Chile and in neighboring countries. After privatization the asset value of Chile's infrastructure companies has grown at a rapid pace, much faster than the overall rate of economic growth (table 4.4).

Favorable business conditions have also been important to attract investors from Chile and abroad for the concession system that is being applied to develop road infrastructure. Low political risks and high credit ratings in international financial markets have facilitated private participation in long-term projects (see case study on roads and transportation).

Strengthening competition

Promoting fair competition is a general policy principle for all infrastructure sectors in Chile, since it is the best way of ensuring efficient operation and better services to consumers. Chile was a pioneer in deregulating its power and telecommunications industries within a competitive framework. There are no restrictions on investors wishing to enter the market nor on customers, who may choose among different suppliers. As a result, capacity shortage has been completely eliminated, the most modern technology is being used, prices have gone down, and companies are still earning fair returns (see case studies on electricity and telecommunications).

It is important to stress that no state guarantees or privileges are involved in telecommunications or power projects. Companies develop projects at their own risk, estimating demand, setting prices, and negotiating with financial institutions. Price regulation applies only to small customers for services in markets where there are natural monopolies, such as telephone services and electricity distribution.

A similar policy has recently been adopted to develop the natural gas industry, supplied by pipelines from Argentina. An open and competitive framework is allowing rapid development

Table 4.4 Asset value of selected privatized companies in Chile, 1987–96

Year	Compañía de Teléfonos de Chile		Entel		Chilgener	
	Assets (US$ millions)	Increase (percent)	Assets (US$ millions)	Increase (percent)	Assets (pesos millions)	Increase (percent)
1987	507	—	139	—	n.a.	n.a.
1988	754	48.7	154	10.8	n.a.	n.a.
1989	975	29.3	209	35.7	n.a.	n.a.
1990	1,379	41.4	259	23.9	n.a.	n.a.
1991	1,688	22.4	301	16.2	408,515	n.a.
1992	2,124	25.8	362	20.3	460,326	12.7
1993	2,481	16.8	394	8.8	605,245	31.5
1994	3,065	23.5	533	35.3	643,063	6.2
1995	3,658	19.3	644	20.8	669,895	4.2
1996[a]	—	—	—	—	781,484	16.7

— Not available.
n.a. Not applicable.
a. As of September 30, 1996.
Source: CTC; Melo and Serra 1996; Chilgener *Estrategia,* November 25 and December 16, 1996.

of this industry, with no involvement by the national governments in project selection or financing. Equal access is guaranteed to all customers requiring gas transportation services provided by pipeline owners, and there are no constraints on investors wanting to build and operate new gas pipelines.

New legislation is being introduced to create a fair and competitive environment in the port and water supply and sanitation sectors that will allow private companies to provide most of the investment required with adequate safeguards for consumers. In the case of ports, the large state-owned company Emporchi will be divided into ten separate, autonomous companies, which will be allowed to compete among themselves and to attract private capital for infrastructure expansion. In the case of water and sanitation, new legislation will allow privatization of state-owned enterprises, within a regulatory framework that promotes efficient operation and marginal cost pricing (see case study on water supply).

In the case of roads and other transportation infrastructure, the state has kept a key planning role but grants concessions to private parties allowing them to build and operate infrastructure and charge user fees. This newly introduced concession system ensures a competitive, transparent, and open bidding process that allows the best projects to be chosen. The only state guarantee is one safeguarding minimum earnings from user charges (see case study on roads and transportation).

Protecting the environment

Environmental protection has become a major political priority in recent years. New norms and legislation have been approved to provide clear rules to investors and ensure that all infrastructure projects are developed in a sustainable manner. Preventing environmental damage is the reigning principle.

A clearly defined review process, with fixed deadlines for final authorization, has recently been established, including detailed regulations. It requires environmental impact assessment studies for most large projects, indicating any mitigation measures required. Many large projects undertaken in recent years have performed such studies on a voluntary basis even when not required to do so by law. Environmental studies are reviewed by an ad hoc technical committee composed of representatives from public institutions involved. The National Commission for the Environment (Conama) or its regional offices, depending on the project's coverage, makes the final decision about the project's environmental feasibility. Third parties that are affected by the projects may file comments during the review process.

Some infrastructure projects need to meet specific environmental and safety standards, such as emissions standards for air and liquid pollutants, quality norms for construction materials, and route design constraints for roads and pipes. Such standards are usually based on international experience.

Satisfying basic social needs

It is a government objective to provide basic social infrastructure to all Chileans. Yet existing policy recognizes that it may be unprofitable for private investors to serve isolated areas or low-income groups. To overcome these limitations the government provides funds for projects that meet minimum social and economic targets. Most infrastructure projects that the government will finance in the next few years would very likely not be developed by the private sector because of low profitability or because it is difficult to charge users.

Mechanisms have been introduced to maximize provision of basic social infrastructure by private investors. Direct subsidies are the preferred measure. For instance, government funds are supplied in a competitive way to private electric and telecommunications utilities that serve rural areas and to ships that serve isolated islands. In the case of water supply and sanitation, the state provides a direct subsidy to poorer families so they can pay the regulated tariffs charged by the companies, which are set at cost. About 20 percent of Chilean families receive this benefit. Mechanisms like these allow poor families to satisfy their basic needs without obliging the state to build or operate infrastructure. The state has only to provide efficient market incentives to private investors.

Ensuring capable state regulation

Private participation does not imply state withdrawal from the infrastructure sector. On the contrary, it requires active and effective involvement of state entities to ensure that private actors operate in line with social goals. To do this, state entities must rely on highly qualified personnel who understand and can implement the regulatory framework. Several state entities are involved in Chilean infrastructure. Ministries dictate government policy and are responsible for the overall performance of specific sectors. The Ministry of Public Works oversees transportation infrastructure (roads, ports, airports), water supply, sanitation, and irrigation. The Ministry of Transport and Telecommunications is responsible for the operation of telecommunications and transportation markets, including urban and intercity traffic, railroads, airlines, and shipping. The National Energy Commission oversees oil, coal, gas, and electricity markets.

Technical and economic regulation is carried out by specialized institutions. There are *superintendencias* for water supply and for electricity and fuels, *subsecretarías* for transport markets and telecommunications, and *direcciones generales* for irrigation, roads, and air transportation. In addition, there is a *fiscalía* (prosecutors' office) and antitrust commissions that monitor competition throughout the economy, including the infrastructure markets. The National Commission for the Environment is responsible for environmental policy and regulation.

The performance of government institutions helps to explain the positive role that the private sector has played in Chilean infrastructure. However, further modernization may be needed to ensure that regulatory duties are performed more efficiently in the future. For that reason the government is promoting administrative and legal reforms in order to strengthen technical capabilities and enhance the power and autonomy of regulatory agencies. Recruitment of highly qualified staff at the regulatory agencies is a main concern. Attractive job opportunities and good salaries in the private sector make it difficult to attract top professionals needed in the public sector. A number of incentives are being considered, including improved salary schemes for regulators and use of external consultants for highly specialized tasks. Another concern has been to give regulatory agencies greater legal authority to ensure enforcement of regulatory norms. Likewise, arbitration mechanisms are being considered for resolution of disputes between agencies and companies that would minimize the need for court litigation.

Private participation in four infrastructure sectors: Case studies

Case studies of the electricity, telecommunications, water supply and sanitation, and roads and transportation sectors describe the process of privatization and the different mechanisms used.

The electricity sector: Wholesale divestiture

In its early stages the development of the Chilean electricity sector was driven almost exclusively by private initiative, but this scenario changed after the Second World War. In 1943 the state-owned company National Electric Company (Endesa) was created by the industrial promotion agency (Corfo) in order to carry out the national electrification plan. Endesa undertook several tasks. It planned the extension of electricity to cover the whole country, studied the availability of hydroelectric resources, trained the people required for the sector's development, built hydro- and thermo-electric generating units in different regions of Chile, extended trunk lines and started interconnecting them, and expanded urban and rural distribution systems. Endesa was a privileged state company and could count on having highly qualified personnel and plentiful resources.

Some private companies coexisted with Endesa but they progressively lost ground. The most important was Chilectra, which produced and distributed electricity in Santiago and Valparaíso and their suburbs. In 1970 Chilectra was nationalized, so by the mid-1970s the state controlled 90 percent of generation capacity, 100 percent of high-tension transmission lines, and 80 percent of distribution systems.

The first step in reforming the electricity sector was taken in 1978 with the creation of the National Energy Commission (CNE). The commission would operate independent of state-owned companies and would promulgate policies, development plans, and regulations for the electricity and other energy sectors. The CNE would lead the reform process in these sectors.

A new electricity law was approved in 1982, establishing an innovative decentralized model for developing the electricity sector, which so far had operated as a vertically integrated, state-owned monopoly. The new approach involved the separation of generation, transmission, and distribution activities; free entry and competition in electricity generation; a concession system for distribution; a marginal cost pricing scheme for small customers, which is reviewed every six months for generation charges and every four years for distribution charges; mandatory interconnection and rights of way for electricity transmission over third-party systems; and a coordination mechanism for load dispatching.

The next step was to prepare the companies for privatization. Chilectra was divided into two distribution companies (Chilectra and Chilquinta) and one generating company (Chilgener). Regional distribution activities and a few smaller generation plants were separated from Endesa to become individual incorporated companies. The largest generation facilities and the transmission lines remained the property of Endesa.

Although care was taken to divide existing companies, the electricity sector remained quite concentrated. Much of the regulatory effort in recent years has been directed to facilitating the entry and operation of new actors in this market. This might not have been necessary had Chile, like some countries that have undertaken privatization recently, been more careful to create a competitive set of companies before divesting to private investors.

In the second half of the 1980s the main power companies were privatized, including Endesa. Open sales of small share packages on the stock exchange were the basic mechanism. The major buyers were the private pension funds, although shares were also offered to employees and civil servants. Shares in electric companies still constitute about half of pension fund investment in private stocks.

The privatization process generated a positive interaction between the power and financial markets. Shares and other financial instruments offered by the electric companies became very attractive in the financial market. The real value of electric companies' shares increased almost one thousand times between 1984 and 1994 and rose from about 2 percent of the total value of shares traded in the early 1980s to more than 45 percent in the early 1990s (table 4.5).

The electric companies also initiated vigorous investment and expansion efforts both in Chile and abroad. Over the past ten years electricity consumption has grown about 8 percent annually, while total annual investment is approaching $800 million. Prices have started to

Table 4.5 Chilean electric company shares traded, 1980–94

Year	Value of electricity company shares traded (1993 pesos millions)	Total value of shares traded (1993 pesos millions)	Electric company shares as percentage of total
1980	3,801	201,669	0.02
1981	1,255	125,816	0.01
1982	1,148	59,062	0.02
1983	1,366	29,6227	0.05
1984	788	23,926	0.03
1985	5,740	34,107	0.17
1986	63,242	192,409	0.33
1987	92,540	309,841	0.30
1988	93,643	373,108	0.25
1989	146,617	468,091	0.31
1990	186,764	394,293	0.47
1991	403,271	904,104	0.45
1992	334,595	884,273	0.38
1993	547,397	1,191,148	0.46
1994	765,019	2,088,827	0.37

Source: Paredes 1995.

Table 4.6 Chilectra's electricity losses, 1983–92
(as percentage of production)

Year	Losses
1983	22.4
1984	19.3
1985	20.4
1986	20.9
1987	19.8
1988	18.8
1989	16.1
1990	13.6
1991	13.3
1992	12.0

Source: Chilectra n.d.

fall as competition in power generation has become stronger and productivity in distribution companies has increased (table 4.6). At the same time the electric companies have become major investors in neighboring countries that have started to deregulate their own electric companies, making use of experience gained operating in deregulated markets. Chilean companies now control between a fourth and a third of installed capacity and distribution in both Argentina and Peru and are starting to invest in Bolivia, Brazil, and Colombia.

The modernization process has received further impetus during the 1990s. The last remaining state-owned power companies have been sold with safeguards ensuring that they would not be acquired by either of Chile's main private generation companies and that they would undertake investment plans to consolidate their competitive position in the market. New norms are also being introduced to improve the regulatory framework, strengthen competition, and ensure that new projects protect the environment. These norms cover the quality of service to be provided by regulated utilities, the fees to be paid by power generating companies using third-party transmission facilities, and environmental impact assessment studies required before building new projects. Mechanisms have been designed to promote investment by private distribution companies in rural electrification projects: state funds are provided in a competi-

tive manner to companies willing to extend the electricity network in rural areas.

A related development that is having a positive effect on the electricity industry is the construction of pipelines across the Andes to bring natural gas from Argentina for combined cycle thermoelectric plants and industrial and residential uses. The idea of building a gas pipeline is very old but has long met resistance for political, economic, and technical reasons. In 1990 the Chilean and Argentine governments called for international bids by private consortia interested in building such a project but had to cancel when they realized that they had no objective way of selecting a winner. The two governments later decided to open the market fully and let private investors take the initiative. This liberal trade agreement granted no exclusivity rights or state guarantees, allowed buyers and sellers to set the terms of the gas supply contracts, and required open access conditions for gas transportation. These conditions set the stage for success. Fierce competition developed between two consortia until one of them was able to sign enough supply contracts with buyers; this consortium will start transporting gas in 1997. The second consortium's project was suspended, but new private projects to build pipelines across the Andes and distribute gas in Chile are being developed.

Telecommunications: Gradual privatization

Telephone service was introduced in Chile as early as 1880, only four years after its invention. In 1927 the main company was acquired by the International Telephone and Telegraph Corporation (ITT), an American corporation, and was incorporated in 1930 as Compañía de Teléfonos de Chile (CTC). CTC soon acquired other, smaller companies and became a virtual monopoly, serving more than 90 percent of the market.

In 1964 the government created a state-owned company, Entel, to provide national and international long-distance services and to represent the country in international agencies such as Intelsat. In 1971 the government took over the management of CTC and in 1974 bought it from ITT. Chile's telecommunications sector was then dominated by a state-owned duopoly, with local services provided by CTC and long-distance services by Entel. Telephone rates were based on long-term average costs, and a 10 percent profit rate was allowed. In practice, however, rates were kept low for political reasons and rate increases frequently failed to keep pace with inflation. There were cross-subsidies in favor of local service. Investment was modest and unsatisfied demand grew.

Reform started in 1977 with the creation of the Subsecretaría de Telecomunicaciones (Subtel), an independent body. Its role was to design policies and technical norms and perform regulatory duties, including the granting of concessions and calculation of tariffs for regulated services.

Box 4.1 Calculating regulated local telephone rates

To calculate regulated local telephone rates, service regions are grouped into a few areas according to demographic parameters. An ideal, state-of-the-art, efficient company serving each of these areas is defined, usually on the basis of proposals from the companies, which are checked by the regulator. In this simulation of a competitive environment prices are calculated on the basis of marginal costs derived from investment and operation costs required for service expansion in line with five-year demand forecasts. The price structure includes fixed and variable charges, with the variable charge depending on the number and duration of calls. The charge per unit of time varies according to the call volume in peak and nonpeak periods of the day. If these charges do not yield the allowed profit rate because of economies of scale, they are adjusted upward, but in such a way as to minimize the resulting reduction in social welfare.

Rates have been set twice according to this procedure, with the second process resulting in a reduction. Telephone companies have continued to invest heavily in the expansion of local service coverage.

The principles of the new regulatory framework were established in the General Law of Telecommunications, approved in 1982 and modified in 1987. The law granted equal rights to private and state-owned companies, within a concession system that allows a company (the concessionaire) to operate providing that it follows a set of well-defined regulations. Prices were freed from regulation except for services that the Antitrust Commission allowed to be provided under monopoly conditions. Free entry to the market was allowed for new companies. Service and interconnection obligations were imposed on telephone companies. Cross-subsidies were eliminated and a long-run marginal cost pricing scheme was introduced for telephone services, with a market profit rate determined by the capital asset pricing model. Prices were to be recalculated every five years, with an index mechanism to be used for the interim (box 4.1).

Privatization of CTC started in 1987, when minority shares were sold to company employees and to pension funds and a request for bids was issued for a 30 percent controlling share with a requirement for continuing investment. An Australian conglomerate, the Bond Corporation, won the bid and then sold its share in 1990 to a Spanish company, Telefónica de España, which remains the controlling investor with 44 percent of shares. In 1989 the state sold its remaining shares in CTC. The private pension funds became important minority shareholders.

The privatization of Entel was conducted slightly differently. Between 1986 and 1990 all shares were sold either on the stock exchange or to company employees. The pension funds were the main buyers. Telefónica de España acquired 20 percent of the company, but after it took control of CTC the Antitrust Commission forced it to divest its share in Entel. Divestiture was completed in 1993. Today Entel is controlled by a partnership formed by the Chilean company Chilquinta and the Italian company STET/Telecom, each holding 19.5 percent of shares, with the pension funds and other groups as minority investors. As a private company, Entel ceased to represent Chile in international telecommunications agencies.

Further reforms were introduced in the 1990s. The law was modified to fully open the market for long-distance services and introduce a multicarrier system allowing any customer to choose among suppliers for each call. Rates have been freed from regulation and new companies have entered the market, making it one of the most competitive in the world.

In addition, a state fund financed by the budget has been created to promote expansion of the telecommunications network to rural areas. Rural communities prepare and propose projects with government help. The projects are usually attractive from a social perspective but not from a commercial one. The fund provides an investment subsidy to make the projects profitable, and private companies compete to receive it. Proposed projects are evaluated by a central council according to their social value. This program is giving hundreds of communities nationwide access to telephone services.

The deregulation and privatization of telecommunications have had very positive results for the Chilean economy. Investment has expanded significantly. The number of telephone lines has more than tripled in eight years, and unsatisfied demand has almost disappeared (table 4.7). New technologies and services have been introduced, and the network has been fully digitized. Companies have diversified their services in both regulated and nonregulated businesses, including cellular telephones, cable TV, and private telephone services. Seven companies offer long-distance services (formerly monopolized by Entel), demand has grown sixfold in the past eight years, and prices have fallen dramatically. Competition is also developing at the local level as new companies have taken on overlapping concessions and ambitious expansion projects. Future plans include technologies such as personal communication systems, which will compete directly with cellular phones in the short run and possibly with local service in the long run, as prices fall as a result of economies of scale and better technology.

Subtel, the state regulator, has played an important role in deregulating the telecommunications sector. It has defined policies and monitored compliance with existing norms. Today one of Subtel's main objectives is to modernize itself in order to improve its regulatory perfor-

mance. State agencies must match the efficiency and productivity improvements of the private sector. One of the main changes being considered is the creation of a superintendency of telecommunications, which would be in charge of monitoring company compliance with regulations and imposing appropriate sanctions, tasks currently performed by Subtel. Subtel would retain responsibility for the political aspects of the telecommunications sector, including the design of laws and regulations, the granting of concessions, and the calculation of regulated rates.

Water supply and sanitation: Private investment, government regulation

Water supply and sanitation services in Chile have traditionally been provided by the state. For many years this task was in the hands of the Ministry of Public Works, through its Directorate for Sanitary Works, and of several municipal and state companies or agencies serving individual cities. There were also a few small private companies that struggled to survive with low, government-set tariffs.

Reform was first attempted in 1977 with the creation of the National Sanitary Works Service (Sendos), which integrated all state institutions involved in water supply and sanitation, including the Directorate for Sanitary Works and the municipal companies. Sendos was an autonomous organization within the Ministry of Public Works that covered the whole country through eleven regional departments. Sanitation services in the two main cities in the country were left in the hands of two state-owned companies: Emos in Santiago and Esval in Valparaíso. The role of Sendos was to plan, build, and operate water supply and sewerage systems, as well as to set quality standards and monitor compliance; the Ministry of the Economy set tariffs. This scheme allowed greater coordination among state units but had its problems, stemming mainly from Sendos's dual role as operator and regulator.

More far-reaching reform was introduced in 1989, when the regulatory role of the state was separated from the operational role of companies, whether state-owned or private. New laws provided the framework for efficient development of water supply and sewerage services

Table 4.7 Chilean telephone service after deregulation, 1987–95

	Lines in service		Telephone density		
Year	Quantity (thousands)	Annual increase (percent)	Lines per 100 inhabitants	Annual increase (percent)	Waiting list[a] (thousands)
1987	581	—	4.65	—	232
1988	631	8.6	4.93	6.0	236
1989	689	9.2	5.40	9.5	284
1990	864	25.4	6.56	21.5	308
1991	1,056	22.2	8.02	22.3	241
1992	1,279	21.1	9.56	19.2	314
1993	1,516	18.5	11.10	16.1	198
1994	1,657	9.3	11.97	7.8	117
1995	1,894	14.3	13.42	12.1	52

— Not available.
a. For CTC, the largest company.
Source: Melo and Serra 1996, based on data from Subtel and company annual reports.

using a concession system, which imposed several regulations on concessionaires. They were allowed to finance operations and investment required for expansion with tariffs set every five years according to marginal cost criteria. A system of direct subsidies for low-income consumers was introduced to offset the impact of higher tariffs and was essential in allowing tariffs to be based on costs. Service obligations and quality norms were imposed on all companies. Compliance with these laws and regulations was ensured by a system of fines and sanctions.

Each of Sendos's eleven regional departments was transformed into a state-owned incorporated company with the same rights and duties as Emos, Esval, and the few remaining private or municipal companies. Regulatory duties were assigned to the Superintendency of Sanitary Services, a newly created body, which was given the right to grant concessions to commercial companies interested in providing water and sewerage services, calculate tariffs, impose sanctions, and regulate and monitor compliance with technical and quality norms. Its head is appointed by the president and has a great deal of autonomy.

The new regulatory model has allowed companies to increase investment in sanitation systems based on earnings, expand water supply and sewerage coverage, and achieve higher profitability (table 4.8).

The current administration has decided to promote further reforms in this sector. In order to achieve 100 percent coverage for water supply and sewerage, undertake major investment in

sewerage treatment plants, and introduce new technologies and managerial skills, much greater private capital participation is required. Therefore, the decision has been made to privatize Emos, Esval, and the regional state-owned companies. A bill was sent to Congress to allow the government to sell up to 65 percent of these companies' shares to private investors. By retaining a 35 percent share, the state will keep some veto power over major corporate decisions.

At the same time, the government has proposed legal reforms that will strengthen the regulatory powers and capabilities of the superintendency. Private control of natural monopolies in the water and sanitation sector will require stronger regulatory authority. Specific norms have been considered to improve the method for calculating tariffs and to restrict horizontal integration of water companies.

Roads and transportation infrastructure: The concession system

The traditional source of financing for construction and maintenance of roads has been the state funds allocated to the budget of the Ministry of Public Works. Tolls for use of intercity roads and taxes on transportation fuels have been charged for many years, but the resulting income has not necessarily been used to extend the transport network. Not surprising, supply has fallen short of demand, and the road deficit has increased. The investment shortfall became more severe in the 1970s and the 1980s, since restricting infrastructure investment was a preferred method for fighting inflation in Chile as in many other Latin American countries. It has been estimated that during the 1980s only 30 percent of road investment needs were met. Road traffic has increased almost fourfold in the past twenty-five years, while the road network has remained nearly unchanged.

In the early 1990s the government realized that the road deficit could become a major bottleneck to economic development. Chile's export-led growth model needed an efficient transport network, since road transit was growing at 9–10 percent annually, and new transport capacity would be required to handle new trade following trade agreements to be signed with neighboring countries. It was estimated that the annual losses due to the road deficit amounted to nearly $1.5 billion, stemming mainly from congestion, pollution, accidents, and load losses due to inadequate transport infrastructure. The government also significantly increased investment in roads, but it became clear that the state would be unable to meet all investment requirements. In order to satisfy the medium-term need for new roads, 1,200 kilometers of roads would need to be paved every year, far more than the 500 kilometers paved by the government in a good year.

The solution was to involve the private sector in obtaining additional funds and also to introduce new managerial practices and technologies. The concessions law approved in 1991 established the framework that would apply for private companies willing to invest in constructing, operating, and maintaining roads and other transportation infrastructure. The concession system involves mainly projects defined by the state. Concessions are granted through a bidding process, with potential investors submitting offers that must satisfy specific conditions stated in the terms of reference. The process is transparent and competitive and does not involve bilateral negotiations. The concession system is flexible and can be applied to roads, ports, and other transportation infrastructure. The law allows private pension funds and insurance companies to invest in the concession projects.

Bids for road concessions are analyzed from both a technical and an economic perspective. Selection is based on such criteria as the

Table 4.8 Performance of the Chilean water and sanitation sector following reform

Investment in sanitation, 1965–95

Period	Investment (1995 US$ millions)
1965–70	71
1971–73	65
1974–89	68
1990–95	151

Urban residents with water and sewerage services, selected years, 1965–95

Year	Urban population (millions)	Water service coverage (percent)	Sewerage service coverage (percent)
1965	5.85	53.5	25.4
1970	6.67	66.5	31.1
1975	7.62	77.4	43.5
1980	8.89	91.4	67.4
1985	9.66	95.2	75.1
1990	11.40	97.4	81.8
1995	11.99	98.6	89.2

Profitability of state-owned water and sewerage companies, 1988–95

Year	Profitability[a]
1988	−1.36
1989	−0.76
1990	−0.82
1991	−0.13
1992	0.94
1993	3.56
1994	5.19
1995	6.30

a. Profits after taxes as percentage of total assets.
Source: Chile, Superintendency of Sanitary Services data.

requested toll level, the tariff structure, the concession period, the subsidy requested or payments committed to the state, the score on the technical evaluation, and environmental considerations. The selected bidder must create a corporation devoted exclusively to the project defined by the bid.

The concessionaire is required to build or improve, operate, and maintain the roads during a concession period lasting no more than fifty years in exchange for toll income. The government usually offers a minimum income guarantee based on traffic assumptions. This guarantee, which is normally accepted by the winning companies, has two main goals: to help the private investor obtain financing and to show the state's commitment to the project. The

Table 4.9 Road and transportation projects offered for concession in Chile, 1993–99
(US$ millions)

Projects	Investment	Amount to be awarded						
		1993	1994	1995	1996	1997	1998	1999
Route 5[a]	1,690	0	0	160	710	820	0	0
Urban concessions	870	0	0	10	250	290	100	220
Interurban concessions	1,533	42	30	381	140	440	500	0
Total	4,093	42	30	551	1,100	1,550	600	220

a. Route 5 is the country's main highway. It is part of the Panamerican Highway System stretching from Alaska to Patagonia.
Source: Chile, Ministry of Public Works 1996.

financial backing is important, since the concession grants only the right to exploit the infrastructure for a given period; the state remains the owner of the road works from the beginning of the project. The income guaranteed by the state usually covers maintenance costs and about 70 percent of operating and capital costs. But if profitability exceeds a previously established level (usually 15 percent), the concessionaire has to share the additional income equally with the state. A conciliation mechanism is available in case of conflicts arising between the investor and the state during the concession period.

Private investors may also propose new projects. If a project is accepted, the company that proposed it receives a bonus in its bid and may receive a full or partial refund of the development costs associated with the project. Many projects have been proposed, several have been accepted (including two airport terminals and urban and interurban roads), and some are being built.

The Ministry of Public Works has created a Concessions Division to regulate the concession system. This division defines projects to be offered, manages the bidding process, and supervises project construction and operation. Regulations governing the concession system and the bidding process have evolved over time. The government has introduced modifications to solve problems as they have arisen, taking into account international experience.

The first concessions were awarded in 1993. Two projects have been finished so far—one tunnel and one road—several more are being built, and others will soon be tendered. The estimated value of projects to be awarded in 1993–99 exceeds $4 billion (table 4.9).

Although it is too soon to evaluate the long-term operational outcome, the Chilean experi-

ence with the concession system has so far been very positive. The private sector, both in Chile and abroad, is highly motivated to invest in roads and other transportation infrastructure that the economy badly needs in order to keep growing. The system allows reduction of the road deficit while freeing government resources for other uses, including the construction of roads that are socially desirable but do not meet minimum commercial conditions to be offered as concessions.

Several factors help to explain the positive response from private investors to concession projects, even if the expected profitability is not high. Internationally, the country is assessed as one with low political risk and institutional and macroeconomic stability. The Ministry of Public Works has carefully overseen thorough preparation of the required studies and undertaken broad promotional efforts. Investors also cannot have failed to notice the steadily increasing demand for this type of infrastructure, which can be expected to keep pace with the economy's sustained growth.

Conclusion

Chile has come a long way in deregulating and privatizing its infrastructure sectors. The private sector is now involved not only in financing investment projects but also in planning, building, and operating new infrastructure facilities. Such participation is guided by general principles, including promoting investment, ensuring fair competition, protecting the environment, and satisfying basic social needs, and by capable regulation.

The current situation owes its success to the design of major reforms that have been introduced over the past twenty years. Generally speaking, sectoral reforms have started with the creation of a regulatory institution to lead the process and of a legal and regulatory framework. The next step has been the privatization of state-owned companies in the case of electricity and telecommunications and the granting of concessions to let the private sector undertake new projects in the case of roads. This sequencing strategy has proved to be effective. Private investment requires clear and stable rules established by law and a regulatory body independent from potential state-owned competitors. Accelerating the process by starting privatization without a proper regulatory framework does not seem to pay off, since high risk will drive away potential investors, and it is difficult to modify regulations once property rights have been awarded.

Private participation in infrastructure has had strongly positive effects on the Chilean economy. Massive private investment has been taking place in energy and telecommunications networks and is starting to flow into the road, water supply, and other infrastructure sectors. Such investment is allowing the economy to maintain high growth rates and the government to use its resources for social objectives. Users have benefited from more and better services at reasonable prices. Companies have increased their productivity, earned fair returns, and diversified their operations in Chile and abroad.

Private participation in infrastructure has posed new challenges for the Chilean government. It has been moving away from managerial activities and has had to develop new regulatory skills. Just as private companies are modernizing and becoming more competitive, the state is reshaping itself to incorporate the human resources and technology required to ensure efficient private development in infrastructure. Consequently, it is promoting administrative and legal reforms that will strengthen its financial and technical capabilities as well as the power and autonomy of its regulatory agencies.

Note

Alejandro Jadresic is minister president of the National Energy Commission, Chile. He wishes to thank Gaston Held for his valuable help, especially with the case studies, for the fieldwork he performed, and for his useful comments.

References

Acevedo, Roberto, and Juan Errázuriz. 1994. "Infraestructura: oportunidad u obstáculo para el desarrollo" (Infrastructure: opportunity or obstacle for development). In Felipe Larraín, ed., *Chile hacia el 2000: Ideas para el desarrollo* (Chile in the year 2000: Ideas for development). Santiago de Chile: Centro de Estudios Públicos.

Alé, Jorge, and others. 1990. "Estado empresario y privatización en Chile" (Entrepreneurial state and privatization in Chile). Cuadernos Universitarios, Serie Investigaciones 2. Universidad Nacional Andrés Bello, Facultad de Ciencias Económicas y Administrativas, Santiago de Chile.

Chile, Ministry of Public Works. 1996. "Programa general de concesiones" (General concession program). Coordinación General de Concesiones, Santiago de Chile.

Chile, Superintendency of Sanitary Services. 1996. "Memoria anual 1995" (1995 annual report). Santiago de Chile.

Chilectra. n.d. "Chilectra highlights." *Chilectra Metropolitana* (company publication).

Díaz, G.-H., Gonzalo Adolfo, and Mario A. López M. 1996. "Representación y proyección tarifaria de empresas y otras consideraciones en torno a la legislación de servios sanitarios" (Companies' tariff presentations and projections and other issues in water and sanitation services legislation). Universidad de Chile, Departmento de Ingenería, Santiago de Chile.

Fischer, Ronald D. 1995. "Economía de las concesiones viales en Chile" (Economics of road concessions in Chile). Universidad de Chile, Departamento de Ingeniería Industrial, Centro de Economía Aplicada, Santiago de Chile.

Galal, Ahmed, and others. 1994. *Welfare Consequences of Selling Public Enterprises: An Empirical Analysis.* New York: Oxford University Press.

Jadresic, Alejandro. 1993a. "Desregulación económica: avances y tareas pendientes" (Economic deregulation: progress and impending tasks). In Eugenio Lahera, ed., *Cómo mejorar la gestión pública* (How to improve public management). Santiago de Chile: Cieplan/Flasco Foro 90.

———. 1993b. "La transformación de la producción, el crecimiento y la competitividad internacional en la experiencia chilena" (Production transformation, growth and international competitiveness in the Chilean experience). In Studies and Reports of the Economic Commission for for Latin America 84. Santiago de Chile.

Melo, José Ricardo, and Pablo Serra. 1996. "Competencia y regulación en telecomunicaciones: La experiencia chilena" (Competition and regulation in telecommunications: The Chilean experience). Universidad de Chile, Departamento de Ciencias Físicas y Matemáticas, Santiago de Chile.

Paredes, Ricardo. 1995. "El sector eléctrico y el mercado de capitales en Chile" (The electric sector and capital markets in Chile). Paper LC/R 1496. Santiago de Chile: Economic Commission for Latin America.

Rojas Pinaud, Alejandro. 1994. "Experiencias de privatizaciones en Chile: Lan Chile, Entel y CTC" (Privatization experience in Chile: Lan Chile, Entel and CTC). Working paper 2. Universidad Adolfo Ibáñez, Instituto de Economía Política.

Sáez, Raúl E. 1993. "Las privatizaciones de empresas en Chile" (Privatization of companies in Chile). In Oscar Muñoz, ed., *Después de las las privatizaciones: Hacia un estado regulador* (After privatization: Toward a regulatory state). Santiago de Chile: Cieplan.

CHAPTER 5

Managing Environmental and Resettlement Risks and Opportunities in Infrastructure

Bradford S. Gentry

Governments struggle to attract private investors to infrastructure projects and to address the problems created by unresolved environmental or resettlement issues. Private investors are acutely aware of the financial risks to infrastructure projects posed by environmental and resettlement concerns. Examples of how these problems can affect private investment in Asian infrastructure abound in the power, water, and transportation sectors.[1]

The risks associated with environmental and resettlement issues reduce the attractiveness of infrastructure projects. But these problems can also create opportunities for governments to improve local environmental and social conditions cost effectively and for private investors to make money. Privately financed water supply and treatment plants can improve water safety, and longer-term prospects of populations affected by resettlement can be improved, for example.

East Asian governments must consider two fundamental sets of questions as they strive to reduce deterrents to private investment. First, why are private investors concerned about environmental and resettlement risks? What legal, operational, and political risks do environmental and resettlement issues pose to infrastructure projects? How do the impacts of those risks vary across different types of infrastructure projects depending on their location, design, construction, operation, secondary impacts, and political sensitivity? Second, what steps can governments take to make private investors more comfortable with the level of environmental or resettlement risk facing a

project and to help them capture the opportunities to address key issues through private involvement? Before addressing this question, governments must recognize that their role has changed, but not been eliminated or diminished in importance, and that affected communities need to be incorporated into the risk mitigation process.

Governments should then follow five basic steps for managing environmental and resettlement risks and opportunities:

- Identify risks and opportunities through environmental assessments (including resettlement issues) and investor due diligence.
- Assess the relative financial importance of particular risks and opportunities.
- Take advantage of opportunities and mitigate substantial risks through design of the project, the environmental legal framework, and the resettlement plan.
- Allocate the residual risks to the parties best able to manage them (sponsors, governments, development banks, private financiers).
- Implement risk mitigation steps in a timely and effective manner.

Environmental and resettlement risks can be managed and opportunities captured. They must, however, be treated not as a special category of problems but as key objectives.

Environmental and resettlement risks as deterrents to private investment

The goal of any private investor is to find deals that offer predictable and acceptable returns. In the infrastructure sector this search is

Box 5.1 Public opposition to the Bakun hydroelectric project in Malaysia complicates financing

The $5.5 billion Bakun hydroelectric power project has long been opposed by environmental and other nongovernmental organizations (NGOs). The dam is designed to provide 2,400 megawatts of power to peninsular Malaysia through a 650-kilometer long undersea cable from the state of Sarawak on the island of Borneo. Located deep in the jungle, the dam would reportedly flood an area the size of Singapore and force more than 9,000 local tribespeople to relocate.

Although the Sarawak government offered to provide new homes or more than $120 million in compensation to those being moved, three of the people to be relocated filed suit, challenging the government's approval of the environmental impact assessment (EIA) for the project.

In its ruling the High Court found that the national government had violated the National Environmental Quality Act by transferring responsibility for approving the EIA to the state authorities in Sarawak (a shareholder in the project).

Differences in federal and state procedure meant that the transfer had the effect of eliminating plaintiffs' right to participate in the EIA process. The court ruled that Ekran, the developer of the project, had to comply with the national act before it could build the dam. The decision has been appealed to a higher court.

The project is proceeding (the plaintiffs' request that an injunction stopping work be issued was denied by the Appeals Court). But the search for financing (a large part of which is reportedly to be secured by floating shares in the dam's operating company) has been made more difficult by the suit, and financial analysts believe that the legal issues must be resolved before financing can take place. In addition, ABB, the construction contractor for the dam, has been the subject of a petition drive by more than a hundred NGOs and thirty members of the European Parliament seeking its withdrawal from the project. Friends of the Earth has also said that it will step up its lobbying of investors in ABB and Ekran.

complicated by the long timeframes over which returns are earned and the "public" nature (and hence political sensitivity) of the services provided. The level of risk inherent in such long-term, sensitive investments leads financiers to address as many significant risks at the outset as they can.

Environmental and resettlement issues can create enormous uncertainty for investors. They can increase completion risk through delays, failure to obtain necessary authorizations, and cancellation in the face of public opposition. They can increase project risk by increasing construction or operating costs, reducing future revenue streams, or decreasing the value of collateral. In extreme cases they can pose direct risks to financiers through liability or the commercial impact of international protests.

Public opposition to infrastructure projects because of environmental and resettlement concerns is now finding its way into the courts in East Asia, further increasing uncertainty for investors. In June 1996 the Kuala Lumpur High Court ruled that the government's approval of the environmental impact assessment for the Bakun hydroelectric project in Sarawak was illegal (box 5.1). Delays to the project would cost almost $4 million a day, according to the chairman of the project company.

Types of environmental and resettlement risks

The environmental and resettlement risks facing any project fall into three main categories: legal, operational, and political.

Legal risks

Legal risks arise when a project is not in compliance with all applicable procedures and standards, including both local laws and the contractual requirements of investors. If the project does not meet local requirements, it may be subject to delays, enforcement, lawsuits, closure, or cancellation. If the project does not meet both local and investor requirements, its chances of attracting international financial support are substantially diminished.

National environmental requirements are often extensive, with regulations setting environmental assessment procedures, project siting approval processes, environmental standards for project operation, and liability for environmental damage. National resettlement requirements in East Asia tend to be less developed than elsewhere, and many countries in the region lack adequate laws on compensation for the taking of private lands or fail to enforce them. Only one country in the region (China)

Box 5.2 The World Bank's pollution prevention and abatement handbook

In 1995 the World Bank released a draft handbook on the environmental performance of the industrial projects it supports (World Bank 1995). Commonly referenced by public and private international financiers, the handbook includes suggested emission limits for different types of projects. The limits for thermal power stations, for example, cover air emissions, liquid effluent, and solid waste. Recommended monitoring and reporting systems are also included.

Box 5.3 World Bank criteria for resettlement plans

The World Bank's directive on involuntary resettlement (Operational Directive 4.30) applies to Bank support of infrastructure projects that use public eminent domain powers to acquire land, whether private investors are involved or not. It includes the following list of factors to be addressed by governments:
- Organizational responsibilities.
- Valuation of and compensation for lost assets.
- Identification of vulnerable groups.
- Resettlement finance and budgeting.
- Community participation.
- Land tenure, acquisition, and transfer.
- Integration with host populations.
- Training, employment, and credit.
- Socioeconomic survey.
- Shelter, infrastructure, and services.
- Legal framework.
- Environmental protection and management.
- Alternative sites and selection.
- Implementation schedule and monitoring.

has a legal framework for addressing the broader social issues created by involuntary resettlement.

The search for support from multilateral development banks brings with it the need to meet additional environmental and resettlement requirements, such as those implemented by the World Bank (Operational Directives 4.01 on environmental assessment, 4.20 on indigenous peoples, and 4.30 on involuntary resettlement). These requirements have been adopted, in large part, to address the criticisms leveled by environmental NGOs and others over the development banks' historical lack of sensitivity to environmental and resettlement issues.

In some cases these standards parallel local requirements; in many cases they go beyond national laws. Included are guidelines for environmental and resettlement review procedures, minimum environmental performance standards (box 5.2), areas to be addressed in resettlement action plans (box 5.3), and public notice and consultation.

Although some countries have raised sovereignty objections to the existence of international standards, their use is on the rise. The U.S. Export-Import Bank and the Overseas Private Investment Corporation (OPIC) have adopted environmental procedures and standards similar to those of the World Bank. In 1995 OPIC took steps to cancel the political risk insurance it had issued to Freeport-McMoRan because of the scope of the environmental impacts from the company's Irian Jaya copper and gold mine. Other national export credit agencies are under increasing pressure to follow the lead of the U.S. Export-Import Bank and apply similar standards to their export assistance programs.

Even more important is the growing number of commercial bankers and underwriters who look beyond local law to international standards on environmental and resettlement issues. The starting point for a commercial banker's analysis is determining whether a project is in compliance with local law, whether or not the law is ever enforced in practice. In countries in which enforcement is lacking, pressure from the financial community to improve compliance represents a new and powerful inducement to meet local requirements at the outset of a project. Many bankers, particularly those from industrial countries, then consider compliance with international standards, which is necessary when development bank support is sought. Even where such support in not sought, however, compliance with international standards is increasingly viewed as a useful defense in the face of international protests over a private investor's involvement in a particular project (see box 5.15).

Operational risks

Operational risks reflect the technical and managerial capacity of the project team to meet the necessary standards. The level of risk depends

---

Box 5.4 Environmental protests delay construction of light rail in Bangkok

Environmental protests have added to the delays and costs facing the already complicated efforts to build three mass transit lines to help ease Bangkok's chronic traffic problems. Two of the lines have been sponsored by Thai developers (Tanayong and Bangkok Land), and one has been sponsored by a Hong Kong (China) firm (Hopewell Holdings).

In response to public pressure to move underground to reduce noise and visual impacts, the Thai government has imposed numerous conditions on the projects, including the commissioning of additional environmental studies and the increased use of underground routes. The furthest along project, Tanayong, has had to move its main depot to a new location as a result of environmental protests. Difficulties in resolving environmental issues and frequent changes in Thai government policy on transport projects have substantially increased the difficulties facing private investors in these projects.

Box 5.5 Resettlement issues delay transport projects in Guangzhou, China

Guangzhou, southern China's most prosperous city, has attracted considerable private interest in transportation projects, although resettlement issues have been a continuing source of controversy. Resettlement compensation was raised as part of the city's efforts to reach agreement with Hopewell Holdings, a Hong Kong (China) firm, for the East-South-West Ring Road, a toll road project that has been stalled by disagreements over investment costs. Significant delays have been experienced over the resettlement of more than 140,000 residents affected by Metro subway line number one.

---

on the ability of the facility to meet applicable standards at the commencement of operations (Has it been properly designed? Does the equipment work as planned? Was the resettlement plan properly implemented?) and the ability of the operator to provide reliable performance over time (Are trained personnel and management systems in place? Are the required actions being taken?). Operating risks are usually less worrisome to investors than legal or political risks, because operating companies tend to be experienced, the level of risk can be assessed by technical consultants, and contractual protections and insurance can be secured.

Political risks

Political risks, which include the risk of opposition to the project and the risk of major changes to the laws governing project construction or operation, are usually the most worrisome to private investors in long-term infrastructure projects. Public opposition is the most unpredictable risk. Most of the other environmental and resettlement issues can be efficiently addressed by project sponsors and the government if they are well managed and sufficient resources are marshaled.

Environmental and resettlement issues are among the most likely to generate significant local or international opposition and press coverage. The intensity of the opposition depends not only on the characteristics of the project but also on the way it is handled. Problems can be exacerbated if the government and the sponsors do not demonstrate a willingness to understand and address local and international concerns, at least to some degree. This is particularly true for resettlement issues.

Public opposition can increase both completion and project risks by delaying a project, raising project costs as a result of required design changes, increasing the possibility that the government will cancel the project, reducing the number of potential investors, impairing the operator's ability to maintain or collect adequate user fees, and, in extreme cases, placing project facilities and personnel at physical risk. Examples of some of these effects can be found in transport projects in Bangkok, Thailand, and Guangzhou, China (boxes 5.4 and 5.5).

Changes in the law, particularly in rules affecting a project's financial performance, are also a major concern to investors. Sometimes referred to as "creeping nationalization," this risk involves unanticipated changes by the government to the rules governing the project that reduce the expected return to investors. Of greatest concern are reductions in the level of fees charged to users. Protests over expressway tolls in Indonesia and Malaysia and sewerage fees in Malaysia have complicated private sector involvement and lowered returns to investors (box 5.6). Unexpected tightening of the environmental standards or widening of the

---

Box 5.6 Protests over sewerage fees force rollback in Malaysia

Since it was awarded the national sewerage concession in 1993, Indah Water Konsortium (IWK) has faced a storm of protest over the fees it charges. The result has been government-ordered reductions and substantial disruptions in getting the business up and running, both of which have fueled continuing protests over the lack of improvement in services.

Before the concession was awarded, sewerage services were the responsibility of 144 separate local authorities, and fees were included in the general local rates. Operational performance was poor and underinvestment in infrastructure was a serious problem. As the government struggled to find an answer to the growing concern over sewage pollution, IWK proposed a national concession. The concession was approved by the legislature, and a new regulatory framework was established for IWK's fees.

Protests over the new sewerage charges began almost immediately. Commercial users of water found themselves confronted with substantial bills for sewerage services, regardless of the quantity or quality of their effluent. No corresponding reductions in local rates were made, and no immediate improvements in service were apparent to the public.

In response to the protests, the government reduced commercial fees over the first three years of the concession, in effect phasing in the new charges. Although this reduction quieted some of the public opposition, fee and service issues have continued to dog IWK. In late May 1996 the company placed full-page ads in all major newspapers announcing a complete review of its operations, including the possibility of further reductions in fees.

---

scope of resettlement efforts may have similar effects by raising project costs.

Effects of environmental and resettlement risks on different types of infrastructure projects

The environmental and resettlement risks facing an investment depend on the following factors, which vary from sector to sector, project to project, and location to location: the sites chosen for both main and ancillary facilities; the design, including expected emissions and other impacts; construction; operation of the completed facilities; secondary impacts, including opening up new areas to development; and political sensitivity over the type of service provided or project undertaken. The nature and intensity of environmental and resettlement issues varies across types of infrastructure projects (table 5.1).

Site selection raises a host of difficult issues, particularly for hydropower, highway, rail (box 5.7), and ancillary thermal power facilities, including fuel source, fuel transportation, and power transmission. The need to resettle residents is a major factor in most of these cases. Flooding of wilderness areas for hydropower facilities destroys forests and biodiversity. Cultural, religious, or archaeological sites and wildlife areas may also be affected. All of these issues raise significant legal, operational, and political risks.

Plant design determines the environmental impacts of facility operations as well as the number of people to be relocated. Air pollution control issues are most pressing for coal-fired power stations, given the concerns over the impact of dust on local health; the effects of acid gases on local health, buildings, and ecosystems; and the impact

---

Box 5.7 Government fails to meet international standards in dealing with relocation issues in Manila

One of the major unresolved issues facing the EDSA Light Rail Transit Project in Manila (LRT 3) is the need to move at least 17,000 squatters from the site on which a depot is to be built. A portion of the site has been cleared of commercial premises through a series of lawsuits and eviction notices. Efforts to relocate the squatters residing on the site began in fall 1995 and had not been resolved by 1996. Part of the delay stems from the difficulty of finding acceptable sites for resettlement. The site preferred by the government is twenty-five kilometers from the depot site and relatively inexpensive. The other possible site is six kilometers from the depot site, abuts a garbage dump, is more costly, and would require more time to prepare. Residents have reportedly rejected the first site.

The government's approach to the resettlement problem did not meet evolving international norms. In particular, the government failed to undertake a comprehensive socioeconomic survey, including a survey of residents' attitudes on a wider range of resettlement options; systematically solicit public input on the resettlement plan; consider acceptable resettlement alternatives, including those providing comparable access to employment, infrastructure, and services; and offer measures to help protect the welfare of the affected families during and for a period after resettlement.

Table 5.1 Relative importance of environmental risks to various types of infrastructure projects

	Thermal power	Hydropower	Renewable power	Drinking water	Sewerage	Highway	Rail
Site selection							
Main facility	✓	✓✓✓	✓	✓	✓✓	✓✓✓	✓✓✓
Ancillary facilities	✓✓✓	✓✓	✓✓	✓	✓✓	✓	✓
Plant design							
Air	✓✓✓					✓✓	
Water	✓	✓✓✓		✓✓✓	✓✓✓	✓	✓
Waste	✓✓				✓✓✓		
Noise	✓	✓	✓			✓✓✓	✓✓✓
Health and safety	✓✓	✓	✓	✓	✓	✓✓✓	✓✓✓
Construction							
Air	✓	✓	✓	✓	✓	✓✓	✓✓
Water	✓	✓	✓	✓	✓	✓✓	✓✓
Waste	✓	✓	✓	✓	✓	✓	✓
Noise	✓	✓	✓	✓	✓	✓✓	✓✓
Operations							
Management	✓✓✓	✓✓✓	✓	✓✓✓	✓✓✓	✓	✓
Health and safety	✓✓	✓✓	✓	✓	✓	✓	✓✓
Emergencies	✓	✓✓		✓✓✓	✓✓	✓✓	✓✓
Secondary impacts	✓	✓✓✓	✓			✓✓✓	✓
Political sensitivity	✓✓	✓✓✓	✓	✓✓✓	✓✓✓	✓✓	✓✓

Note: Intensity of risk is indicated by number of checks.

of carbon dioxide on global warming (box 5.8). Water quality issues are critical to the operations of water and hydroelectric facilities. The need to dispose of sewage sludge creates major waste issues for sewerage systems. Noise is a major factor in transportation projects and presents at least some risk to most other projects as well.

Construction generates significant environmental impacts, which are usually temporary and manageable by qualified contractors. These risks are thus largely operational risks. During operations the quality of management's implementation of the environmental and resettlement programs is key to the success of the project. Failure to implement a well-designed operations or resettlement plan increases the risks to private investors. Emergencies—such as release of toxic materials—are a particular concern in drinking water systems, where operational risks are usually the principal concern. Secondary impacts range from the ancillary development spurred by the opening of highways into new areas to the increases in consumption of resources that often accompany expanded access to power or roads. These impacts generally increase legal risks in the structuring of the project or political risks over its life.

The *political sensitivity* of different types of projects is critical and affects all aspects of project preparation and implementation. For projects that have come under the public spotlight—locally or internationally—new hurdles to project completion are erected (table 5.2).

A cooperative approach to environmental and resettlement issues

All of these environmental and resettlement issues can be managed once government accepts that increased private involvement in infrastructure means that its role has only changed, rather than been eliminated or even diminished in importance, and that public involvement is critical. While governments no longer have primary funding or operating responsibility, they set targets and frameworks for private involvement at the outset and have an ongoing responsibility to monitor performance and apply frameworks in a predictable and consistent manner over the life of the project. This changed role affects both project design and regulatory oversight activities. Effectively meeting these new responsibilities means that the government and the private operator have to build a long-

Box 5.8 Japan and China work together to develop cleaner coal

A unique set of relationships is emerging between China and Japan as they struggle through the environmental and economic implications of the rapid expansion of coal-fired power stations in China.

The internal debate over increased coal use is intensifying in China. In March 1996 the federal cabinet released a report to the National People's Congress stating that the coal sector must "accelerate production to meet the country's increasing energy demands." In April 1996 the Chinese Ministry of Public Health and the State Science and Technology Commission reported that pollution was now a leading cause of illness and death in many Chinese cities and that air pollution, much of it caused by the burning of coal, was of particular concern. Similar results from earlier studies led a Standing Committee of the National People's Congress to call for much tighter controls on sulfur dioxide emissions in the fall of 1995. The government was thus faced with the need to both increase coal production and reduce air pollution, something it could achieve only by investing in air pollution controls.

Japan has many reasons to try to help China reduce the environmental impacts of its expanding power sector. Concern that acid rain from China is damaging Japanese forests is growing. Japan is a leading exporter of air pollution control equipment, and the Chinese market is potentially huge. Japanese companies are also seeking to participate in the growth of private sector involvement in Chinese infrastructure and other projects.

The result has been a number of "cleaner coal" initiatives in China sponsored by the Japanese government. As part of its "green aid" program, the Japanese Ministry of International Trade and Industry has been demonstrating the use of lower-priced flue gas desulferization equipment in a small number of Chinese power plants. In 1996 the Japanese Overseas Economic Cooperation Fund announced that it was focusing its new special loan program to China on environmental projects, including cleaner coal usage, and formal agreement among China, Japan, and Germany was expected on the cosponsoring of a feasibility study for a coal liquefaction plant (expected to cost $500–$600 million).

Table 5.2 Politically sensitive issues that can affect infrastructure projects

Issue	Types of projects particularly affected
Resettlement of large numbers of people, particularly indigenous peoples or squatters (box 5.1).	Hydropower facilities, highways, and rail lines.
Imposition of new or significantly increased user fees on "public" services (box 5.6).	Water supply or wastewater treatment, roads, and electricity.
Destruction of large areas of tropical forest or other sensitive habitats (box 5.14).	Hydropower facilities.
Emission of large quantities of air pollutants affecting local, regional, and global environmental conditions (box 5.9).	Coal-fired power stations.

term working relationship based on clearly defined roles. While each has its own areas of exclusive responsibility—with the government responsible for regulation and the operator responsible for technical performance—joint action will be necessary on many issues, including major resettlement issues. Since it is impossible to anticipate and provide for all contingencies that may arise over the course of a twenty-year concession, the parties must develop a strong working relationship based on respect and understanding of each other's goals. Lessons from experience in developing such working relationships are now beginning to emerge from earlier privatization efforts, such as that in Buenos Aires (box 5.10).

Since public opposition is often the most unpredictable and worrisome risk facing infra-structure projects, the public must be involved in the risk mitigation process early and often. Such involvement can provide early warning concerning project features that might lead to opposition and help establish ongoing relationships with the community, which would allow the sponsor to monitor and respond to new issues as they develop.

Public involvement is a sensitive, complicated, and uncertain process. In some countries public criticism of government-supported projects is actively discouraged; in others there has been little experience in soliciting public input. Identifying and reaching the various groups to be consulted can be difficult. Deciding how much public involvement is enough and what changes should be made to project design requires judgment.

Box 5.9 Public opposition to coal-fired power plants suspends construction in Thailand

During the 1990s a number of coal-fired power plants became the subject of environmental protests in Thailand. One of the earliest was the Mae Moh station, in northern Thailand. In October 1992 adverse weather conditions and a malfunction at the plant created an air pollution event that caused hundreds of residents to require treatment for respiratory problems. As a result the Electricity Generation Authority of Thailand had to cut back production at the plant, reducing its already strained total generating capacity by 3 percent.

In early 1996 construction of an experimental power station was suspended by the government following protests by local residents. Designed primarily to burn municipal solid waste, the plant had also planned to use coal for up to 40 percent of its fuel in its early years.

Although project sponsors may fear that informing the public may delay or even derail a project, experience has shown that effective public outreach minimizes the risk of significant public opposition and saves time and money over the life of the project. In Calcutta, India, for example, an outreach program involving private investors successfully developed a resettlement plan (box 5.11). Some multinational companies view public involvement as the means of obtaining the "social license to operate," which they regard as just as necessary as any legally required permits.

Addressing environmental and resettlement issues is a continuing process that involves both private and public parties. A five-step process consisting of identifying, assessing, minimizing, allocating, and implementing can be adopted. Activities in any one of these areas are affected by activities in the others and usually proceed in parallel.

Identifying potential environmental and resettlement risks and opportunities

The process of identifying environmental and resettlement risks and opportunities must begin at the earliest stages of project development, and it must continue throughout the life of the project. As new parties become involved in the transaction, they should be brought into the process. Once the government has identified its

---

Box 5.10 Developing a good working relationship in Buenos Aires: Aguas Argentinas and ETOSS

Aspects of the 1993 privatization of the Buenos Aires water system demonstrate the importance of clearly defined roles and long-term working relationships. Clear standards of performance were established and a pricing structure that encourages efficient operation was adopted. A regulatory body, Ente Tripartito de Obras y Servicios Sanitarios (ETOSS), was created to oversee the activities of the concessionaire, Aguas Argentinas, and a variety of procedures are being used to resolve disputes between the parties. More important, however, as the concession goes on, each party is beginning to understand the other's goals and methods of operation more clearly. As the parties work through the wide variety of issues that arise through daily operations, a track record is being established that helps build trust. As Aguas collects and makes available to government authorities more data on regional environmental conditions, the government is more likely to seek input from the company on regional environmental planning. While this may eventually raise questions of "regulatory capture," it provides the parties with a basis for cooperating to resolve problems they both face.

---

goals for the infrastructure investment, it should undertake the initial analysis during preparation of terms of reference. In the case of an unsolicited bid, the sponsor should do so. Once the concession has been awarded, the process should continue jointly between the government and the sponsors, with the involvement of financiers before closing. The project operator should then carry the effort forward, with input from the government and the affected public.

One of the first steps will be the commissioning and execution of some form of environmental impact assessment, often accompanied by or incorporating resettlement issues (box 5.12). Such reviews are almost always required under national law and by development banks. Where private developers are involved, they are usually responsible for preparing the environmental impact assessment. Failure to conduct an adequate assessment provides project opponents with a powerful device with which to delay the project, as demonstrated by experiences in Malaysia, the United States, and Europe.

Once the environmental impact assessment has been conducted, other types of risk of concern to private investors can be identified. For legal risks all applicable requirements must be identified and their likelihood of being met assessed. Performing such an assessment requires both legal and technical skills and is usually handled by local and international law firms working closely with engineering consultants. In many countries it is difficult to find local lawyers familiar with both environmental requirements and the needs of private investors. As both local and international law firms gain experience with these issues, however, these difficulties are diminishing. The sponsor's advisers usually take the lead on these issues, subject to confirmatory analysis by the lenders' advisers.

Identifying operational risks requires assessment of the technical and managerial capacity of the project to meet the required standards. The sponsor's personnel, working closely with its suppliers, will prepare a plan for doing so. Their plan is then reviewed by the government's technical consultants and then by technical consultants retained by the lenders. Many engineering firms are qualified to review these plans, although the different cost pressures facing the design and operation of privately financed facilities may make assessments difficult for consulting engineers whose only experience is on public sector projects.

The methods for identifying political risks—particularly the likelihood of significant public opposition—are the least well defined, because the issues themselves are less clear. The first step is for international sponsors and lenders to engage in a broad effort to try to understand the country and its politics, goals, and needs. Sponsors then work with government officials to identify the risks facing a particular project.

Public outreach is an extremely important part of this effort. Ideally, such efforts begin with the environmental impact assessment. The basic features of an outreach program include the following:
- Identifying affected groups (both local and international) through contacts with government, community, environmental, religious, business, and other organizations.
- Providing notice of the proposed project, including a project description, through media bulletins, local project offices, interested organizations, and community meetings.
- Offering opportunities for concerned citizens to submit comments on the project through written remarks, surveys, individual interviews, focus groups, and public meetings.
- Analyzing and developing responses to the comments received, by making changes to the project or explaining why requested changes will not be made.
- Disseminating the responses to the affected groups through media bulletins, local project offices, interested organizations, community meetings, and revised project descriptions.

- Engaging in an ongoing process of providing information and receiving public input on the project, through local project offices, mailings, community meetings, and citizen advisory boards.

Assessing the significance of particular risks

After environmental and resettlement risks and opportunities are identified, their significance to the project needs to be determined. First, a rough order of magnitude must be estimated for the financial implications of each risk or opportunity. In some cases this is a relatively easy task; in other cases assigning a financial value is complicated. For example, it is difficult to determine the cost of the delays incurred as a result of disturbances at sites with local historical or religious significance. Measuring and valuing these impacts can be difficult. Doing so is necessary, however, to give both government sponsors and private investors a basis for deciding whether or not to proceed with the transaction.

Second, the available estimates must be compared with the value of the deal as a whole or the ultimate costs to users. Although the cost of mitigating a risk or capturing an opportunity may seem large in absolute terms, it may represent an insignificant amount in the context of the overall deal. Calculating possible impacts on user fees or investors' return allows sponsors and the government to decide whether or not to go forward and to focus their efforts on those risks and opportunities with the greatest potential impact on the deal.

Minimizing risks during project design

The most effective time for governments and private investors to consider environmental and resettlement issues is at the earliest stages of project design. By including environmental and resettlement goals from the beginning, governments can bring private sector creativity to the design of cost-effective solutions. Private investors are most comfortable when clear investment targets are presented and significant risks can be eliminated through careful project development.

In order to make the most of the project design phase, governments must pay special attention to their overall infrastructure goals and the range of methods for meeting them, the environmental regulatory framework adopted for the project, and the plan to be developed and followed for addressing any involuntary resettlement issues.

Infrastructure goals and alternative methods for meeting them. Government infrastructure planning has historically focused on large, high capital cost facilities, often designed without substantial attention to environmental or social impacts. As governments seek to increase the private sector role in such projects, they often use these prior infrastructure planning efforts and assumptions as the basis for bids and other private involvement.

By relying on earlier planning efforts, governments often miss out on opportunities to apply private sector resources and creativity to the cost-effective attainment of environmental and development goals. This is true for two major reasons. First, only relatively recently have environmental and resettlement issues begun to have a major impact on infrastructure planning efforts. Second, while the private sector can often meet many of the government's infrastructure goals more cost effectively and more reliably, its ability to do so is severely constrained if it is limited to working within the confines of early public sector plans.

To capture opportunities for improving environmental or social conditions through private involvement, governments need to take two steps. First, they should assign higher priority to a wider range of environmental and resettlement goals. These targets can then be included in the optimization process for developing alternative approaches to meeting infrastructure needs. Clean water is already a priority for most countries in East Asia. Greater priority should be given to increasing the efficiency of power use and controlling dust and acid gas emissions from thermal power stations. Opportunities for ancillary environmental benefits for highway projects should be valued more highly. In cases of involuntary resettlement, alternatives that minimize the numbers of people moved or maximize the social gains to those affected should be weighted more heavily.

If governments set environmental and social targets, private investors will respond with methods and prices for meeting them, providing governments with a measure of the cost of achieving these targets. Broader consideration of environmental and resettlement goals will also help reduce the potential for local and international public opposition. In turn, this will expand the pool of potential international funding sources.

Second, governments need to be willing and able to consider a wider range of methods for meeting their goals. The clearer governments can be about goals and the more leeway they can give the private sector to design methods for meeting them, the more likely the private sector is to come up with cost-effective solutions. Choosing among a range of options, however, requires a broader range of skills than that demanded by the traditional approach of putting a publicly designed power plant out to bid.

Allowing the private sector flexibility to develop solutions may lead to recommendations on different aspects of projects:

- *Types of projects.* If the goal is to make 800 megawatts of power available, a combined offer to provide 700 megawatts of new generating capacity with 100 megawatts of measurable energy conservation gains might better meet the joint power and environmental goals at a lower cost (box 5.13).
- *Locations for projects.* It may be possible to reconfigure the design of hydroelectric facilities or transportation corridors in order to minimize the amount of land affected or the need for resettlement.
- *Technical designs.* Both Aguas Argentinas (the operator of the privatized water and sewerage system in Buenos Aires) and the Indah Water Konsortium (the national sewerage concessionaire in Malaysia) were able to design sewerage systems that met the performance standards set by the government for much less than estimated in earlier government plans.
- *Operating practices.* Experience with coal washing in the United States and Australia demonstrates that substantial economic and environmental benefits can be achieved as a result of reduced ash content (reducing both transportation costs and emissions) and

Box 5.13 Adopting a demand side management approach to energy efficiency in Thailand

In 1991 Thailand became the first Asian country to adopt a utility-sponsored demand side management (DSM) energy efficiency program. A 1995 review of the potential for investment in Thailand's energy efficiency industry by the International Institute for Energy Conservation documents the wisdom of this initiative.

On average Thai investments in increased energy efficiency cost less than half the price of new generating capacity for the same level of megawatts. An achievable DSM potential of at least 2,000 megawatts over the next decade has been identified—25 percent of planned system expansion. As much as $2.3 billion in capital costs could be saved if an aggressive program to capture 2,000 megawatts of peak demand was in place. Foreign operators with extensive experience with DSM programs in other markets (especially the United States) can readily bring this knowledge to bear in Thailand, helping to capture these opportunities.

increased combustion efficiencies (China is seeking to increase the amount of coal it washes from 24 to 30 percent by the end of the century).

- *Financing packages.* The $30 million grant from the Global Environment Facility to the Leyte-Luzon geothermal project in the Philippines is one example of the public financing benefits that can accompany the design of projects with an increased "environmental increment."

The choice of projects still rests with the government. Recognizing and making explicit the trade-offs made in the final selection of a project is an important part of the process of minimizing public opposition. In some cases the importance of a particular project for meeting the government's goals must be made clear in order to secure international financial backing. The proposed $1.2 billion Nam Theun II hydropower project illustrates many of the issues facing efforts to increase private involvement in politically sensitive "spotlight" infrastructure projects (box 5.14).

Environmental regulatory frameworks. Governments need to establish and work within clear, predictable, and reliable frameworks for overseeing private sector environmental performance. Clear rules allow investors to price and design projects to reflect environmental concerns. Governments

Box 5.14 Addressing the concerns of the international financial community over the Nam Theun hydroelectric project in the Lao People's Democratic Republic

The Nam Theun II project is designed to export 681 megawatts of power to Thailand in return for much needed foreign exchange. Gross revenues to the Lao government are expected to rise from $10 million to well over $100 million a year (in constant 1994 dollars) over the twenty-five-year concession term, doubling foreign exchange earnings and increasing GDP by 20 percent.

The new dam would flood approximately 450 square kilometers, 30 percent of which is forested and rich in biodiversity. In addition, 900 poor households would need to be relocated from the reservoir area. Several thousand people in the catchment area, along the reservoir perimeter, and in the downstream channel area would also be affected by the project.

These environmental and resettlement problems have led to local and international opposition to the project. Environmental organizations have opposed the loss of forests on the Nakai Plateau; others have protested the resettlement plans. The intensity of these objections has been increased by the international spotlight on large hydropower projects in Asia (Three Gorges, Narmada, Bakun) as well as by the protests over implementation of the environmental mitigation plan for the Pak Mun hydro project in Thailand.

The project is also financially risky. The projected cost is equivalent to about 75 percent of the country's 1994 GNP and neither the Lao People's Democratic Republic nor the private sponsors (Transfield of Australia, Electricité de France, and Italian-Thai and Phatra Thanakit of Thailand) have the resources to undertake the project alone. International finance is thus necessary. Crafting a project attractive to international financiers requires that environmental and resettlement issues

be addressed in a manner acceptable to the international financial community. In most industrial countries, private investors will not invest without development bank support; the World Bank cannot provide that support unless environmental and resettlement issues are addressed to its satisfaction.

To address these concerns, the government needs to make clear why hydropower is critical to meeting the development needs of both the Lao People's Democratic Republic and Thailand and why it opted to develop hydropower rather than other sources of power, such as nuclear or coal-fired stations.

The project also needs to be designed to optimize economic, environmental, and resettlement benefits over the long term. This will require a commitment by the Lao government to ensure implementation of the environmental and resettlement programs. Efforts are under way to offset the loss of forests in the flooded area with much greater protection of a larger forest preserve within the project's catchment basin. In addition, a more extensive resettlement plan is being considered that would allow the local population to share in the economic benefits of the project. Taking such efforts together, the project may result in more effective protection of a large tract of rain forest.

All of these issues are now under consideration by project sponsors and the government. Support for the project has been received from two international environmental NGOs (the Wildlife Conservation Society and the World Conservation Union), and the possibility of involving the United Nations Development Programme's local office in the outreach necessary for development of the resettlement plan has been discussed.

---

can then decide if the cost of compliance is too high. If the rules are not clear or if they are inconsistently applied, private investors will assign a higher risk premium to environmental issues, resulting in higher than necessary project costs.

An "ideal" environmental regulatory framework for an infrastructure project consists of an integrated package of laws and contracts that specifies the following:

- Standards of performance (set in terms of simple emission limits and other readily measurable factors) that leave the private operator the flexibility to determining how to meet the standards.
- Relationship of current and future environmental performance standards to the level and regulation of user fees, particularly in light of fees previously charged (or not) by the government for such services.

- Environmental review procedures to be followed.
- Administrative procedures to be followed by the government in deciding on authorizations for the project, including mechanisms for contesting aspects of the government's decision.
- Monitoring, reporting, and inspection procedures to be followed, including the role (if any) of the public and of NGOs.
- Sanctions to be applied in the event of nonperformance or environmental damage, including identification of all parties that may impose the sanctions, the procedures for doing so, and the mechanisms for contesting the sanctions.
- Remedies available to the private operator, if any, in the event the government changes environmental standards in the future.

Given such a framework private investors can build environmental considerations into project design, internal environmental management systems, community outreach programs, subcontracts with suppliers, insurance, and other project components.

Requiring private investors to meet such standards need not mean that projects will be too expensive or will fail to attract investors. In fact, two of *Asia Money*'s 1995 project finance "deals of the year" were power stations that successfully met the environmental standards applied by both the national governments and the U.S. Export-Import Bank (box 5.15).

Resettlement plans. Reducing the risk of public opposition through fair and equitable treatment of the affected populations should be the cornerstone of risk management from a project's inception. Minimizing risks to investors goes hand in hand with minimizing risks to people affected by the project.

The process should begin with a clear definition of the tasks and responsibilities assigned to different parties in the deal. This can be done though a combination of national laws and contracts. The resulting package of responsibilities should cover the following areas:

- Preparation of the resettlement plan, including the items to be covered and standards to be followed in doing so.
- Acquisition of the land to be taken for both the project and the relocated people.
- Relocation of the affected people.
- Economic rehabilitation of the affected people, both those relocated and those otherwise affected by the project.
- Monitoring and supervision of implementation of the resettlement plan.
- Mechanisms for resolving disputes on resettlement matters, including those between the government and the affected people and those between the government and the private sponsors or investors.

Where truly voluntary resettlement (wholly consensual purchases of the necessary land at open market prices) is involved, the private sponsors of the project will be able to take the lead in relocating the affected parties. Where involuntary resettlement is involved, however,

> **Box 5.15 Meeting the environmental standards of the U.S. Export-Import Bank: The Paiton I (Indonesia) and Sual (Philippines) power projects**
>
> Two large power projects were financed with the help of the international financial community. No significant public opposition to the projects was raised, and all of the international institutions involved were satisfied that environmental standards had been met.
>
> The $2.5 billion Paiton I project involves two baseload 615-megawatt coal-fired power units in northeast Java, Indonesia. The U.S. Export-Import Bank provided political risk cover for a $540 million loan. The U.S. Overseas Private Investment Corporation (OPIC) provided $200 million in financing. The $1.35 billion Sual project involves a 1,200-megawatt coal-fired station in the Pangasinan province of the Philippines. The U.S. Export-Import Bank guaranteed more than $370 million in debt, and the International Finance Corporation (IFC) provided both direct loans and syndication of commercial bank debt.
>
> The U.S. Export-Import Bank, OPIC, and the IFC all apply their own procedural and substantive environmental standards to the projects they support. In addition, two of the commercial banks involved in these deals—Chase Manhattan and Citibank—confirmed that they look to such "world" standards for comfort as part of their due diligence on the environmental risks facing power projects.

governments need to take the lead, especially in cases involving involuntary resettlement of large numbers of people, including squatters and indigenous peoples. Private investors are less equipped to handle involuntary resettlement issues because they are often unfamiliar with local conditions and lack credibility among the local population. Moreover, the political risks of leaving involuntary resettlement in private hands are considerable and could increase the level of resettlement payment.

International investors are extremely reluctant to commit financing to a project until involuntary resettlement issues are addressed, even if the government provides complete cover for the financial risks posed. For example, at least one international investor active in power projects has decided not to pursue the Ib Valley project in India, in part because the new project has revitalized old, unresolved resettlement claims in the area.

The forcible clearing of a site by the government is not likely to address international investors' concerns, particularly when viewed

---

Box 5.16 Major findings of the World Bank resettlement review

Involuntary resettlement is almost always more difficult, more expensive, and more time consuming than governments expect, according to the World Bank (1994). Several factors appear to explain the differences between successful and unsuccessful resettlement efforts:

- *Strong political commitment.* The adoption of legal frameworks and guidelines (regional or sectoral) for resettlement is an early expression of political commitment. Conscientious and timely implementation of those rules (particularly the payment of compensation or provision of replacement land) confirms that commitment.
- *Focus on income restoration.* Creating the conditions for successful income restoration is critical to resettlement efforts. Achieving this goal is enhanced when the affected parties share in the immediate benefits of the project. Moving affected parties to newly pro-

ductive areas created by the project, favoring them in project hiring and ancillary developments, and assisting them in building improved housing will help mitigate the adverse effects on these people.

- *Accurate costing and financing.* Poor performance on resettlement was often traced to inadequate economic analysis, externalization of re-establishment costs onto the affected population, and underfinancing. In the twenty cases reviewed, resettlement costs averaged 9 percent of appraised costs and went as high as 35 percent.
- *Participation of the affected parties.* Outreach is critical to inform affected populations of the possible need to resettle and to obtain their input on sustainable solutions to resettlement. Doing so often substantially decreases the likelihood of major public opposition.

---

over the life of a long-term concession, because of the increased likelihood of up-front delays and negative publicity for the project, the creation of local ill will (and the possible effect on the future level and collection of user fees), and increased long-term risks to project facilities, particularly along lengthy corridors.

Lessons from government efforts to address the risks of involuntary resettlement can be found in the World Bank's 1994 resettlement review, in which the Bank reviewed resettlement experience in 192 projects it financed between 1986 and 1993, with a combined displacement of 2.5 million people (boxes 5.16 and 5.17). The International Finance Corporation (IFC) conducted a similar review in 1995. The IFC had been involved in only seven resettlement projects, affecting only about 2,500 people. Virtually all of the IFC's projects involved private sponsors leading voluntary resettlement efforts at negotiated market prices.

These and other experiences with involuntary resettlement suggest that the government needs to develop and implement, with input from affected parties, a resettlement plan that addresses public concerns while meeting government and investor goals. To do so, the government should take the following steps:

- Coordinate development of and commit to implementing a comprehensive resettlement plan (with support from private sponsors).

- Begin community outreach as early as possible, preferably before a final siting decision is made, and involve local groups in the communities the affected people will be moving from and to.
- Consider how to address the different needs of the parties being relocated, particularly property owners, squatters (including later waves of squatters), and indigenous peoples.
- Develop plans to address both the replacement of housing (either directly or through payment of compensation) and long-term income restoration (through jobs on the project and training, for example).
- Seek opportunities to upgrade local infrastructure, housing, landscaping, and similar amenities as part of the resettlement package.
- Establish adequate mechanisms for recourse by affected parties that wish to challenge the government action.
- Prepare complete and accurate cost estimates for the full resettlement plan.
- Secure adequate financing (from both public and private sources) for different components of the plan.
- Adopt community-based mechanisms for monitoring and implementing the plan.

Once the government takes these steps, private parties can make technical, operating, and financial support available for different parts of the plan at different times.

Box 5.17 Resettlement lessons from China

In its 1994 review of government-sponsored resettlement efforts, the World Bank concluded that "resettlement in China is now generally considered to work well and even adds to project benefits" (page 4/16). Four major reasons were given by the Bank for this apparent success:

1. *Incentives.* Resettlers receive strong incentives to move, ranging from increased living space to significant compensation payments.
2. *Decentralization.* Responsibility for resettlement, including development and implementation, is at the local or city government level.
3. *Institutional policies and procedures.* China has adopted binding policies and procedures for agriculture, energy, and urban development projects, expenditures on which are reviewed by national auditors.
4. *Giving resettlers a stake.* Resettlement efforts hinge on providing productive resources to new communities, with many communities using the opportunity to launch new enterprises they previously could not afford.

Table 5.3 Responsibility for residual environmental and resettlement risks

Risk	Host country	Sponsor	Development banks	Private financiers
Meeting legal standards				
Environment		1	3	
Resettlement	1	2	3	
Operational				
Technical		1		
Managerial		1		
Political				
Local opposition	1	1	2	3
International opposition	1	1	2	3
Fee collection	1	2	2[a]	3
Change in law	1			

Note: 1 = party usually takes the lead in addressing or bearing risk.
   2 = party often bears a portion of the risk and works actively to address it.
   3 = party usually provides technical support on or actively monitors the level of the risk borne by other parties.
a. If guaranteed.

Allocating residual risks to the parties best able to manage them

While the goal of risk management is to eliminate as many risks as possible during design, significant risks always remain. Residual risks need to be allocated to the parties in the best position to manage them. This is usually done through the contracts that make up the project and financing documents.

Environmental and resettlement risks are allocated among the government, project sponsors (including their subcontractors), development banks, and private investors (table 5.3).

Different parties are best able to manage particular risks. Private parties are well positioned to address risks involving technical and operational issues and to provide support for community relations activities. Governments are best placed to bear political risks, including the risks associated with many aspects of resettlement. Development banks can provide technical assistance and direct support in the event of significant international public opposition as well as guarantees of government obligations under certain circumstances. Private financiers are extremely risk averse and will want essentially all project risks allocated to other parties before providing funding. After the deal is signed, private financiers will monitor only those issues having an obvious and direct impact on borrowers' finances or a potential impact on their other operations. However these responsibilities are allocated, assignment of risk needs to be clear. Risks should not remain unaddressed because they were unassigned in the contract.

A clear process for responding to unanticipated risks also needs to be in place. Much of the success of such efforts will stem from the quality of the relationship established between the government and the sponsors. In addition, the contracts and regulatory framework should spell out clear mechanisms for identifying key, unresolved issues, resolving issues at higher levels of management, and using arbitration or other mechanisms to resolve outstanding issues.

Implementing risk management programs

From a private investor's perspective, failing to implement a risk management program is just as bad as not having developed a plan in the first place, because it gives opponents grounds on which to attack the project. Protests over the performance of the Pak Mun hydropower project in Thailand (including the alleged negative impact on the fishing industry and the poor implementation of the environmental mitigation plans) demonstrate these difficulties.

Conclusion

The environmental and resettlement issues associated with infrastructure projects represent both risks and opportunities. The challenge facing governments is to bring the power of the private sector to bear on priority environmental and social issues. For many government officials this will require a change in the traditional view that economic development and environmental protection are fundamentally inconsistent with each other. This view leads to efforts to exclude environmental considerations from the goals of development policies, including planning for infrastructure projects. The result is projects that lack clear guidance for investors on environmental issues and that are more likely to attract public opposition. Similar problems often accompany resettlement issues, particularly where indigenous peoples or squatters are affected.

The first step in meeting this challenge is to convince development ministries that it is in their best political interest to take environmental and resettlement issues seriously from the very beginning of infrastructure planning efforts. Doing so can improve the health and productivity of local citizens, reduce the uncertainties—and hence costs—facing private investors, and extend the efficiency gains from private involvement in infrastructure services. Private investors will participate in projects with a higher environmental or social content if the targets are clear. Governments will know the true costs of such alternative approaches only if they solicit bids based on meeting environmental and resettlement targets.

The second step is to build the capacity of governments to evaluate and oversee private activity aimed at meeting environmental and social targets. Private companies will meet only those targets that have a significant impact on their commercial interests. If governments set targets but have no basis for evaluating private proposals to meet them, the effort will fail. Effective mechanisms for monitoring performance must also be in place.

Setting, evaluating, and enforcing targets for private sector activity are among the core activities of governments in their changed role in infra-structure. Including environmental and resettlement considerations among the priority factors to be optimized during infrastructure planning will help ensure that opportunities are captured, risks mitigated, private investment increased, and development benefits maximized.

Notes

Bradford S. Gentry is director, Research Program on Private Finance and the Environment, Yale Center for Environmental Law and Policy.

1. Examples include the Bakun and Nam Theun II hydropower projects, the Malaysian sewerage concession, and the Bangkok and Manila light rail projects.

References

International Institute for Energy Conservation. 1995. *Thailand's Energy-Efficiency Industry: Potential for Investment.* Washington, D.C.

World Bank. 1994. *Resettlement and Development: The Bankwide Review of Projects Involving Involuntary Resettlement.* Washington, D.C.

———. 1995. "Mainstreaming the Environment." Washington, D.C.

CHAPTER 6

Financing Private Infrastructure: Lessons from India

Montek S. Ahluwalia

The infrastructure requirements of East and South Asia are very large and are increasing rapidly because of strong economic growth. Countries throughout the region have recognized that the public sector is unlikely to mobilize the required resources and that the private sector must be brought in as a supplementary source of finance. Private sector participation in infrastructure is desirable not only to ensure a larger flow of resources but also to introduce greater efficiency in the supply of these services.

The explosion of global capital markets and the associated expansion of private capital flows to emerging market economies provide new opportunities to finance infrastructure projects in these countries, if projects can be made commercially viable. Several experienced international companies are interested in investing in infrastructure development in Asia provided the overall investment climate is perceived as attractive, and many countries in the region have domestic entrepreneurs keen to enter these sectors.

Despite these apparently favorable circumstances, the experience in introducing private investment into infrastructure development has been mixed at best. There have been some notable successes in East Asia, but the pace of implementation in many countries, especially in South Asia, has been much slower than was initially expected. The slow pace has not reflected the lack of private capital. Although the resources available are probably inadequate to meet all of the infrastructure needs of the region, which are indeed enormous, fewer private sector projects are currently being financed than are feasible with current levels of resource availability. In other words, the operative constraint is not the level of resource availability but the ability to structure projects in a manner suitable for private financing.

This chapter examines the reasons why so many developing countries have experienced difficulties in implementing private sector infrastructure projects. It focuses on problems associated with the fact that infrastructure projects are generally subject to tariff regulation, which presents special problems for private investment; the nature of the risks associated with infrastructure projects and the consequent need for complex risk mitigation arrangements to ensure financeability; and the need to mobilize a suitable mix of finance, especially long-term finance, which is not easily obtained.

The problem of tariff determination

Tariffs on all infrastructure projects are regulated; private operators are not free to fix or adjust tariffs at will. The tariff is typically fixed in advance and adjustable over time only in accordance with predetermined contractual terms. Private investment can be attracted into a tariff-regulated sector only if investors are convinced that tariffs will be set and periodically adjusted in a manner that ensures an adequate rate of return to investors. Equally important, the public utility character of infrastructure projects requires that the tariff be perceived as "fair" to consumers. This balance is not always easy to strike, and disputes over tariffs can delay project implementation. Some of the alternative ways of fixing remunerative tariffs, and the problems associated with them, are discussed in the following sections.

Cost-based tariffs

The traditional approach to fixing tariffs that are both remunerative and reasonable is to tie the tariff to normative levels of costs per unit for given levels of capacity and production. These cost-based tariffs cover capital costs on the basis of approved levels of capital expenditure and variable costs on the basis of specified parameters of operating efficiency. They also include a component for return on capital, which is calibrated to yield an acceptable rate of return to investors at a reasonable level of capacity utilization and operating efficiency. Cost-based tariff formulas generally include explicit provisions for adjustment of tariffs over time to reflect rising prices.[1] This cost-based approach to utility pricing has been used to price electric power supplied by independent producers to a monopoly distributor. It has also been used to determine tolls for roads, bridges, and bypasses.

The cost-based approach has many problems. From the point of view of the producer, the attractiveness of the tariff depends on whether the rate of return on equity generated by applying the cost-based formula is sufficiently remunerative for investors. Experience suggests that private investors in infrastructure projects in developing countries typically expect rates of return on equity of 20–25 percent. This is much higher than the rates of return normally used for determining public sector tariffs. China initially capped rates of return in the power sector at 15 percent, deterring many investors. The cap has since been relaxed. In India the rate of return normally used to fix tariffs for public sector power producers is 12 percent after tax. In order to attract private investment the return on equity was raised to 16 percent at 68.5 percent capacity utilization, with incentives that yielded additional returns of 10–12 percentage points for capacity utilization of 85 percent. However, in the Indian tariff formula these rates of return accrue only from the date of commercial production; no return accrues during construction. The internal rate of return on equity, which takes into account the lack of return during the con-

struction period, is therefore much lower. Private power producers have accepted this formula only because the operational efficiency norms used in computing variable costs are relatively lax, and most private power producers expect to improve on these norms, thereby achieving internal rates of return of more than 20 percent. The formula has been criticized on this count as being nontransparent.

Cost-based formulas are generally vulnerable to the criticism that the approved capital costs are excessively high or the efficiency norms excessively lax. There is no transparent way of countering this criticism. Estimates of capital costs are especially difficult to defend against suspicion of cost padding or "gold plating" of capacity. This problem is especially acute when equipment suppliers belong to the project sponsor group. Comparison with costs of other public sector projects is one way of determining whether costs are appropriate, but such comparisons ignore differences in technology and quality. For example, high capital costs in private sector power projects may be associated with greater fuel efficiency, which reduces the power tariff. All these issues, as well as issues connected with risk mitigation, have surfaced in one form or another in the public debate over the cost of private power in India (box 6.1).

Tariffs and competitive bidding

An alternative approach to fixing tariffs is competitive bidding. Relevant technical and production characteristics of the project are specified in advance, and qualified bidders are asked to bid in terms of the lowest tariff at which they would be willing to undertake the project. As in the case of cost-based tariffs, these tariffs have to be adjusted over time to reflect inflation, and the manner in which this adjustment will be made must be specified in the invitation to bid. Under this approach cost padding is not a problem, and there is a transparent way of determining the lowest tariff at which the project can be implemented. If existing public sector suppliers are also allowed to bid competitively, the approach establishes a level playing field for the private and public sectors and thus ensures least-cost supply for individual plants. High rates of return

Box 6.1 India's experience with the power sector

India announced a new policy for attracting private sector investors in power generation in 1992. The policy envisaged bulk sale of power to the state electricity boards at negotiated rates based on a cost-plus formula. A large number of memorandums of understanding were signed, involving 80,000 megawatts of additional capacity. Implementation has been much more modest.

Problems of tariff determination and risk mitigation proved more complex than envisaged at the time the policy was announced:

- The cost-plus formula was perceived as being vulnerable to padding of capital cost. The same formula had not attracted criticism earlier, when both generating stations and distributors were in the public sector, but the formula was felt to be unacceptable when applied to private sector projects. It became evident that much higher levels of due diligence are expected when there is a public-private interface. The government has since announced that future projects will be awarded on the basis of competitive bidding.

- The policy did not originally envisage any guarantees by the central government, but many private investors were unwilling to accept assurances of payment for power purchased by the state electricity boards because of their poor financial condition. Moreover, they were not satisfied with guarantees given by the state governments and insisted on counterguarantees from the central government. The central government ultimately decided to extend such counterguarantees for the first eight private sector projects.

- Private investors sought much greater risk mitigation than public sector players had. Private investors looked for exchange risk protection, assured off-take of power subject to plant availability, protection against fuel supply risk, and other risk mitigation schemes. These special features were criticized in the public debate as being excessively favorable to private sector projects.

- The first power project sponsored by the Enron Corporation at Dabhol in the State of Maharashtra ran into a series of hurdles, including renegotiation of the initial agreement, because of a change in the state government. It also faced several legal challenges in public interest litigations, including challenges of the validity of environmental clearances. Fortunately, these obstacles, including twenty-five court cases, have been overcome, and the project is currently under construction.

The complexities involved in achieving financeable packages for private sector power projects were not adequately appreciated at the outset. As a result, resolution of problems, involving interaction with several government agencies, took time. The government ultimately appointed a high-level board consisting of senior representatives of the various ministries involved to resolve problems.

Progress has recently accelerated. The 700-megawatt Enron project at Dabhol is under construction, and two power projects have actually started generating power (the 235-megawatt GVK project at Jegurupadu in Andhra Pradesh and the 208-megawatt Spectrum project at Kakinada in Andhra Pradesh).

---

realized by investors in a competitive bidding framework need not attract controversy, since the bidding process ensures that the tariff is the lowest possible. High returns under these conditions can only reflect increased efficiency, which should be encouraged.

One limitation of the competitive bidding approach is that transparency in bidding requires full specification of the minimum technical requirements of the projects, which calls for considerable advance work before bids are solicited. Certain characteristics of the project, including basic technical specifications and the expected level of guaranteed supply, must be specified. Environmental regulations may also impose certain conditions with which all bidders must comply. However, it is important to avoid overspecifying technical details to the point of foreclosing technology choices, which

are best made by private investors searching for least-cost solutions.

Competitive bidding also has its limitations. A bidding process will yield the lowest cost option only if enough qualified bidders actively compete. In practice the number of bidders for an infrastructure project may be limited, for several reasons. Lack of information and clarity about various aspects of government policy relevant to the project may deter many eligible bidders from bidding. This may occur if the legal, financial, and technical requirements of the project are not spelled out in advance or there is lack of confidence that the integrity of the bidding process will be maintained (that is, the predetermined requirements will not be changed after bids have been solicited). In such situations fixing tariffs through competitive bidding could produce an outcome inferior to that that could have been achieved through negotiations. An International Finance Corporation study (1996) comparing tariffs in different power projects in Indonesia concluded that there was no evidence that tariffs arrived at through competitive bidding were lower than tariffs fixed through negotiation. The experience in the Philippines leads to the opposite inference. Tariffs in the earliest power projects, which were set on a negotiated basis, were as high as 8 cents a kilowatt hour; tariffs on the later projects, which were competitively bid, were as low as 5 cents a kilowatt hour.

In the final analysis the relative merits of fixing tariffs through competitive bidding or negotiation will depend on the quality of the bidding process in the one case and the quality of the negotiating process in the other. Negotiation may well yield a better outcome in some cases, but competitive bidding is more transparent, an overwhelmingly important consideration in government decisionmaking. On balance competitive bidding is superior to negotiation, and most developing countries have adopted this approach where possible.

Regulated tariffs with competitive bidding

In many situations tariffs are not determined by competitive bidding but are fixed by a regulatory or other authority. In such cases competition can be used to select the private investor by soliciting competitive bids in terms of the license fee offered during the concession period or in terms of a revenue-sharing arrangement. This approach is particularly well suited to cases in which the independent producer deals directly with the final consumer and demand forecasts ensure profitable operation. In telecommunications, for example, there is often significant unsatisfied demand at prevailing tariff levels, and new licensees can expect to be profitable within a relatively short time.[2] A similar situation may obtain in port development, where capacity may be visibly overstrained and private sector investors may be willing to expand port facilities or set up new competing ports, subject to a common tariff fixed by a regulatory agency. The Jawaharlal Nehru Port Trust in India recently awarded a $200 million port expansion, involving private sector construction and operation of two new container

terminals, to an Australian-Malaysian joint venture through competitive bidding on the basis of revenue sharing.

The license fee or revenue-sharing approach can be adopted wherever the licensee can make sufficient profit to be able to offer a license fee or a share in revenue. In other situations, such as construction of toll roads with low traffic projections in the initial years, it is not possible to ensure profitability with any plausible tariff for many years. In such cases private sector investment is possible only if returns to investors can be enhanced. The simplest solution is to offer an operating subsidy, or an up-front capital subsidy, with the subsidy determined by investors bidding competitively for the lowest subsidy. A second approach is to bundle an existing public sector asset into the concession to increase the profitability of the new investment. In India, for example, the government has announced that private investors will be invited to invest in widening two-lane toll-free roads into four-lane toll roads. The inclusion of the two-lane road, with its established traffic flow, provides a larger and more certain return, making competitive bidding possible. A third approach is to include other commercially profitable opportunities, such as commercial development of real estate in areas opened up by a new road, as part of the project. This internalizes benefits generated by the project, improving the attractiveness of the investment and making competitive bidding possible. A variant of this approach is to delink the infrastructure component of the project from the exploitation of associated profit-making opportunities and to solicit competitive bids for each separately. Explicit subsidies can then be provided for the infrastructure component, financed by revenues realized from the profitable component. In Hong Kong, for example, the real estate development rights over each station on the rail link between the city center and the new airport have been bid out competitively, and the revenues generated will be used to finance the airport.

Public acceptance of tariffs

Any of these methods of fixing tariffs can ensure adequate returns to investors. More difficult is ensuring that the resulting tariffs pass the test of public acceptance. Private sector suppliers will often require higher tariffs than those being charged in the public sector system, because public sector supplies of urban services, roads, and even power, are typically heavily underpriced, reflecting large subsidies. The switch from underpriced public sector services to fully priced—and therefore more expensive—private sector services can generate resistance from consumers.[3]

Higher-priced services from the private sector may not be resisted if the private sector is seen as providing an additional, and perhaps higher quality, source of supply, with consumers retaining the choice to continue with the existing lower-quality public sector service. Introduction of a new privately operated toll highway as a higher-priced but faster alternative to a publicly maintained toll-free road may not evoke consumer resistance, for example. However, conversion of toll-free road into a toll road could meet with stiff resistance.[4] The difference in consumer reaction to private entry into telecommunications and electricity generation in India illustrates the problem. Consumers showed no resistance to the entry of new private sector cellular telephone service providers, which offered a higher-cost service that competed with the fixed public sector phone service. In contrast, the entry of independent power producers selling power to the state electricity boards, which then distribute power to final consumers, did meet with some resistance. Although the tariff charged by independent power producers to the state electricity boards does not directly affect the tariff charged by the boards to final consumers, there was concern that reliance on higher-priced private sector power would raise the average cost of the state electricity boards, which would eventually lead to higher prices for consumers.

Is such consumer resistance justified? The answer clearly depends on whether the cheaper public sector supply reflects greater efficiency compared with the private sector alternative or merely reflects its subsidization by the government. In most cases low public sector tariffs reflect large subsidies, either explicit (through the budget) or more often hidden (in the form of public sector losses). Consumers pay for these subsidies in the form of higher taxation or reduced

levels of expenditure on schools, public health, and other essential services, but this implicit payment is usually not recognized as a cost. Public acceptance of higher tariffs from private sector projects therefore depends crucially on public realization that continuation of subsidized public sector tariffs is simply not feasible. This is indeed the case in most developing countries, since the public sector cannot even ensure continued supply, let alone provide increased supply, at prevailing prices. Indeed, one of the compulsions for seeking private investment in infrastructure development is precisely the lack of public sector resources because of chronic underpricing.

This is not to say that tariff increases by private sector providers should be uncritically accepted. One of the arguments in favor of involving the private sector in infrastructure is that it is likely to be more efficient than the public sector, and it is important to ensure that these efficiency gains are achieved. The cost of services supplied by the private sector should therefore be the lowest possible and should compare favorably with the real economic cost (excluding subsidies) of the public sector alternative. At first glance cost minimization can be ensured by competitive bidding, but if comparison with the public sector alternative is an important benchmark in ensuring public acceptance, competitive bidding is effective only if the public sector also participates in the bidding. The experience of Hyderabad, India, in privatizing the supply of drinking water is instructive in this context. International bids were solicited for a $300 million urban water supply project, and three bids were received. However, the cost of the lowest bid was found to be more than 60 percent higher than the estimated real cost (excluding subsidies) if the project were to be implemented by the public sector. The city authorities decided to reject all bids and opt for the public sector alternative. Cost efficiency of private sector infrastructure projects, including comparison with the public sector alternative, must be a prime consideration in evaluating such projects.

Risk mitigation and private financing

All investment projects involve some risk, but infrastructure projects in developing countries are perceived as unusually vulnerable to risks, which constrains financing. Risks are perceived as high partly because projects are typically undertaken not by established utility companies with strong balance sheets but by special purpose companies executing individual projects on a build-operate-transfer or build-own-operate basis. Project financing is on a nonrecourse basis (that is, lenders do not have recourse to the sponsor company but look solely to the revenue stream of the project available to meet debt service obligations). The risks associated with the revenue stream are therefore scrutinized. Equity investors may be willing to accept higher levels of risk in return for higher expected returns on their equity, but lenders typically have a lower tolerance for risk and a greater need for risk mitigation mechanisms. Although governments conduct project negotiations with the sponsors, it is the lenders behind the scenes who set risk mitigation standards and determine whether projects are financeable.

Different kinds of risk

The general principles for risk mitigation are well known. The various risks involved should be unbundled and assigned to the participants able to manage them at least cost. Risks that can be more efficiently handled by agencies outside the project are shifted to these agencies, thereby reducing the residual risk borne by the project. This process of shifting risks typically involves a cost, which is subsumed in the tariff by the sponsors. If risks have been efficiently assigned to those best able to manage them, the cost of risk management is minimized and the tariff is a minimum-cost tariff.

The major risks involved, the methods for handling these risks, and the problems that can arise in each case are discussed in the following sections. Some of these risks are prevalent in most investment projects. Many are particularly important in infrastructure projects.

Construction risk. Construction risk refers to unexpected developments during the construction period that lead to time and cost overruns or shortfalls in performance parameters of the completed project. High capital intensity and a rela-

tively long construction period make project costs especially vulnerable to delays and cost overruns. As a result construction risk is generally higher in sectors such as power and roads and lower in sectors such as telecommunications and urban services.

Construction risk can be reduced through a variety of instruments. The reputation and experience of the sponsors and the engineering, procurement, and construction contractor is an important element in assessing construction risk. Project sponsors can shift a portion of the construction risk to the contractor through engineering, procurement, and construction contracts that provide for turnkey responsibility, with penalties for delays and shortfalls in performance parameters of the plant on completion. Such performance guarantees add to the cost of the project. While construction risk can be shifted to some extent, it cannot be eliminated entirely, since penalties for nonperformance are typically capped at certain levels and the residual risk has to be borne by investors. However, lenders would be satisfied with risk sharing that reduces project risk to a level that can be absorbed by equity investors without jeopardizing loan repayments.

Operating risk. The technical performance of the project during its operational phase can fall below the levels projected by investors for a number of reasons. Operating risk is usually low for infrastructure projects that rely on a tested technology, as is the case with most power plants and roads. It is higher in sectors in which the technology is untried or is changing rapidly, such as telecommunications. Operating risks are typically mitigated by entrusting operation to experienced operations and maintenance contractors. Contractual arrangements with such contractors can include some provisions for liquidated damages. Many risks during the operational phase, including certain force majeure risks, are commercially insurable, and private investors will typically insure against such risks.

One source of operating risk that is very important in the power sector is fuel supply risk. Power projects are highly vulnerable to interruption of fuel supply, and independent power producers generally seek to shift this risk to the fuel supplier or the purchaser. Private financing of power projects depends critically on the ability to negotiate satisfactory fuel supply agreements, with appropriate penalties payable by the fuel supplier in the event of nonperformance. Fuel supply problems are being tackled in different ways in different private sector power projects in India. The 700-megawatt Dabhol project in Maharashtra relies on imported naphtha, with the fuel supply risk borne largely by an international supplier. The 235-megawatt gas-based GVK project in Andhra Pradesh relies on natural gas supplied by the public sector monopoly supplier. In the event of a fuel interruption, the supplier has the option of switching to more expensive imported naphtha, with the higher fuel cost "passed through" to the tariff. In the 1,040-megawatt Visakhapatnam coal-based power project in Andhra Pradesh, the fuel supplier, Coal India Ltd., is a government-owned company, and coal transportation depends on Indian Railways, which is also government owned. The fuel supply agreements with Coal India Ltd. stipulate substantial liquidated damages, which cover the fixed capital charges and expected returns up to certain levels, in the event of nonsupply. In the 1,000-megawatt Bhadravati power project in Maharashtra, the private producer is developing a private sector captive coal mine to supply coal to the project. The project sponsors are taking on the fuel risk because fuel is being supplied by an associated company.

Market risk. Market risks relate to the possibility that market conditions assumed in determining the viability of the project are not realized. Nonfulfilment of demand projections is an obvious example of market risk. In certain situations investors expect the monopoly purchaser to guarantee a minimum level of purchase, thus eliminating market risk for the investor. This is typically the case when an independent power producer sells power to a monopoly distributor or a water supply project sells water in bulk to a monopoly urban water distributing company. In other cases, such as telecommunications, ports, and roads, in which the private producer deals directly with individual users and users typically face competing options, market risk is borne by the investor.

Investors are expected to undertake market studies and satisfy themselves that market demand projections at feasible levels of tariffs would yield adequate profitability.

The situation in which no reasonable toll-cum-traffic projection can ensure profitability must be distinguished from market risk, which refers to situations in which traffic is projected to be adequate but there is considerable uncertainty in the forecast. Financial projections must allow for downside possibilities. In these situations project sponsors may expect the government to share downside risks through guarantees involving payments to cover part of the earnings forgone if traffic falls below a certain level. To ensure symmetry, such guarantees can be balanced by a corresponding sharing of revenues if traffic exceeds a certain level. In this way part of the risk can be shifted to the government. Although governments are normally reluctant to offer such guarantees, they may well represent the less expensive option if the only alternative is for the entire burden of uncertainty to be borne by the government.

Interest rate risk. Interest rate risks arise because interest rates can vary during the life of the project. They are particularly important in infrastructure projects because of the high capital intensity and long payback periods. High capital intensity implies that interest costs represent a large part of total costs; long payback periods mean that financing must be available over a long period, during which interest rates may change. One way of handling interest rate risk is to pass it on to consumers, as, for example, in arrangements in which the impact of interest rate variations on unit costs are treated as a pass-through into the tariff. In the cost-based tariff formula used in many power projects in India, for example, interest costs are built into the tariff. Such an approach is neither necessary nor desirable, however, since any arrangement that automatically passes on these costs to consumers reduces incentives for cost minimization. An alternative is to allow the risk to be borne by the investor, who in turn can hedge the risk through devices such as interest caps and collars. The feasibility of this option depends on the sophistication of the relevant financial markets and the availability of hedging instruments. Typically, it is much easier to hedge interest rate risks in international markets than in domestic markets, since domestic hedging instruments are not available in most developing countries. The cost of hedging would, of course, have to be borne by the project and reflected in the tariff.

Foreign exchange risk. Two types of foreign exchange risk need to be distinguished. One relates to exchange convertibility, the assurance that revenues generated in domestic currency can be converted into foreign exchange for making payments abroad. This risk must be borne by the government through suitable convertibility guarantees. The other type of risk is exchange rate risk, the risk that exchange rate changes lead to large increases in the domestic currency costs of payments denominated in foreign currency. This risk is extremely important for infrastructure projects that rely heavily on foreign financing but that have tariffs fixed in domestic currency.

Exchange rate risk can be handled in different ways. When the tariff is fixed in foreign currency (as may be the case with port charges) or when it is automatically adjusted to reflect the impact of exchange rate variation on those cost components that are denominated in foreign exchange, exchange rate risk is borne by consumers. In many cases, however, tariffs may be indexed only to domestic inflation, exposing the project to the residual foreign exchange risk. It is not easy to shift foreign exchange risk in such cases. If long-term swaps between domestic and foreign currencies were readily available it would be possible to hedge this risk at a cost. Such swaps are typically not available in most developing countries, however, partly because of inadequate market development and partly because of government policy. Hedging instruments cannot develop as long as foreign exchange markets remain tightly regulated.

The absence of hedging instruments is not the only problem. The inherent uncertainty about exchange rate movements in developing countries is such that even if hedging instruments were to evolve, they would be very expensive. The only way to reduce foreign

exchange risk in this situation is to limit the extent of external financing. This in turn depends on the existence of a healthy domestic capital market capable of providing sufficient domestic financing for infrastructure projects.

Payment risk. Investors in infrastructure also face the risk of not being paid for services delivered. The importance of this risk varies across sectors. It is not very important in projects in which the sponsor deals directly with a multitude of consumers, as in the case of a telephone company, a toll road, or a port. It becomes very important in situations in which an independent power producer has to supply electric power to a monopoly buyer, such as a public sector distributor, or a water purifying company has to supply water to a municipal distributor. Because the financial condition of public sector utilities in developing countries is often very weak, investors are naturally concerned about the risk of nonpayment for power or water delivered to the distributor when the producer has no alternative outlet for the product.

The long-term solution to this problem is to improve the financial standing and creditworthiness of the utilities or to privatize distribution so that private sector suppliers can deal directly with private distribution companies or undertake distribution themselves. Pending such improvement, a variety of alternatives exist. Independent power producers in India have typically sought state government guarantees of payment for power delivered and credit enhancement through a counterguarantee of the state governments' obligations by the central government. Alternatively, they have sought to set up escrow arrangements under which payments due to the utility company from high-quality industrial consumers are placed in escrow accounts for settlement of the dues of the private power producers as a first charge.

Regulatory risk. Regulatory risk arises because infrastructure projects have to interface with various regulatory authorities throughout the life of the project, making them especially vulnerable to regulatory action. Tariff formulas ensuring remunerative pricing at the start of the project can be negated by regulatory authorities on the grounds that the tariff was too high, as happened in the Bangkok Second Expressway and the recent privatization of the water supply in Manila. Problems can arise from the environmental sensitivity of many infrastructure projects. Extensive environmental clearances are usually necessary at the start of the project, but clearances can be challenged in public interest litigation or through direct activism by nongovernmental organizations, which can lead to delays in construction or disruption in operation. The experience of the Dabhol Power Project in the Indian State of Maharashtra exemplifies this problem (see box 6.1). Another source of regulatory risk is that environmental concerns and standards can become more stringent during the life of the project, adding to the costs of operation. Private investors will expect explicit assurances that cost increases imposed because of regulatory action will be reflected in a corresponding adjustment in the tariff to project profitability.

In general, regulatory risk is best handled by establishing strong and independent regulatory authorities that operate with maximum transparency of procedures within a legal framework that provides investors with credible recourse against arbitrary action. This is not simply a matter of setting up new systems and procedures. The systems must be perceived as credible, something that will happen only when sufficient experience is gained about their functioning. Until then risk perception will remain significant.

Political risk. Infrastructure projects have high visibility, and there is always a strong element of public interest. This makes them vulnerable to political action that can interrupt or upset settled commercial terms; in extreme cases it can even lead to cancellation of licenses or nationalization. These risks can be partially mitigated through political risk insurance offered by multilateral organizations, such as the Multilateral Investment Guarantee Agency, or bilateral investment protection agreements. They can also be addressed by building into the project agreement appropriate levels of compensation for arbitrary action, subject to international arbitration. The World Bank's new partial risk guarantee instrument, which covers debt service payments in case they are inter-

rupted because of nonperformance of specific government obligations, is another instrument that can play a useful role in this context.

Arrangements for risk mitigation

The risks enumerated above are not equally important in all projects. The significance of particular risks will differ from project to project, depending upon sector characteristics. Road projects may have high construction risks, low operating risks, and high market risks. Telecommunication projects may have low construction risks but high market risks. Power projects with suitable offtake guarantees may have high construction risks, relatively low operational and market risks, and high payment risk. Each project has its own risk profile, and risk mitigation structures will vary depending on the specific circumstances of each project.

Because of the nature of the risks and the involvement of many participants, including project sponsors, lenders, government agencies, and regulatory authorities, risk mitigation arrangements are usually complex. They involve detailed legal and contractual agreements that specify the obligations of different participants, set forth clear penalties for nonperformance, and offer protection to investors against actions beyond their control. The complexity of these arrangements often delays implementation. Because public sector infrastructure projects do not use such arrangements, host country governments are often unfamiliar with them. For example, public sector power generating companies that purchase fuel from other public sector companies typically do not insist on fuel supply agreements with strict penalty clauses of the type demanded by the private sector. Nor do they insist on power purchase agreements with as much protection in terms of guaranteed commitments to purchase power, incentive payments, and penalties. More generally, public sector interactions for contractual obligations are often loosely defined, with a great deal left to trust rather than laid down in tightly defined, legally binding contracts. Private sector investors cannot be expected to accept this approach. Moreover, a much higher level of due diligence is expected from government agencies in dealing with the private sector.

For all these reasons, the development of satisfactory risk mitigation arrangements is difficult and time consuming. Lack of experience with such arrangements—and inadequate appreciation of their necessity on the part of host governments—can lead to delays that hold back project implementation. These problems are more severe in the early stages and are illustrated by India's experience in trying to attract private sector investment in power generation (box 6.1) and telecommunications (box 6.2).

Costs of risk mitigation

Risk mitigation involves costs, which raises the question of whether private sector projects, which require risk mitigation, are unnecessarily costly compared with public sector projects. The answer depends on whether the risks involved represent real potential costs that have to be borne even if the project is undertaken by the public sector and whether the premium paid for risk mitigation is too high.

Many of the risks that concern private sector investors represent contingencies that should concern public sector projects as well. For example, the risk of a fuel supply interruption is just as great in a public sector project, and the resulting loss of power generation represents a real cost to the project and the economy. Public sector power producers are less concerned with protecting themselves against these risks, partly because they are less concerned with ensuring the commercial profitability of each project and partly because they perceive that shifting these risks to other parts of the public sector would not improve the system as a whole.[5] Risk mitigation in these cases raises the explicit cost of private sector projects, but it does not necessarily make them more costly for the economy as a whole, since the same costs are incurred in public sector projects, whether or not they are made explicit. Explicit assignment of risk to agents better able to manage them could reduce costs if it leads to improved management of risk.

In some situations, however, private sector projects face risks that do not arise in the case of public sector projects. For example, private investors may be concerned about risks stemming from lack of clarity of government policy, the absence of a credible regulatory system, and the possibility of arbitrary political action. High risk perception on these counts leads to high private sector project costs, because many investors are discouraged from exploring investment possibilities, leaving the field to investors willing to live with greater uncertainty in the expectation of higher returns. These high returns are ultimately paid for by the consumer in the form of higher tariffs (or where tariffs are fixed independently, lower license fees accruing to the exchequer). It should be noted, however, that higher costs in these situations are not caused by risk mitigation but arise precisely because risks cannot be mitigated and are traded off against high returns. The aim of policy in such situations should be to reduce perceived risks by introducing greater clarity in government policy and providing an environment that reassures investors. Such an environment, which should include a legal framework for enforcing contractual agreements and independent regulatory authorities to ensure fair treatment, would encourage a larger number of private investors to enter the field. The resulting increase in competition could be expected to reduce the cost at which services are offered.

Sources and methods of financing

Once suitable tariff fixing mechanisms and risk mitigation structures are in place, private sector projects become financeable in principle. At this stage project implementation depends on the ability to develop a financing package with a mix of finance suitable for the project. This mix varies from sector to sector. Telecommunications projects, which face relatively high market risks, may require a relatively low debt component, with debt to equity ratios close to 1:1. Power projects with assured power purchase arrangements may be financeable with debt to equity ratios of 2.5:1 or even 3:1. The maturity requirements of debt will also vary across sectors. Power and roads, which have longer payoff periods, typically require long maturities, while telecommunications projects can manage with shorter maturities. The mix between domestic and external financing also requires careful consideration. Even if external financing is available

---

Box 6.2 Competitive bidding in telecommunications services in India

India's telephone services were run as a public sector monopoly until 1992, when private sector cellular services were allowed to operate in four metropolitan cities (Delhi, Bombay, Calcutta, and Madras). Shortly thereafter both cellular and basic services were opened up for private sector operators in twenty telecommunications circles covering the entire country. Although at each stage private sector operators were chosen through a form of competitive bidding, the process was criticized and challenged in court.

Introduction of cellular services in the four cities was done by soliciting bids from companies short-listed on the basis of qualifying criteria. Call charges were independently fixed, and potential entrants were asked to bid in terms of criteria such as the rental charge on the phone, the extent of domestic equipment purchase, and projections of investment and performance. The weights assigned to each criterion for bid evaluation were not made public. The initial selection of licenses on this basis was challenged in court, and a fresh selection had to be made at the direction of the court.

The bidding process was much more transparent for the extension of cellular and fixed phone services throughout the rest of the country. Eligibility criteria were made public, and bids were solicited for individual circles on the basis of the license fee offered and three other quantifiable criteria. Weights assigned to each criterion were also made public. Potential bidders were even asked to seek clarifications, and all clarifications issued were made public before the final submission of bids. Despite these efforts at transparency, problems persisted:

- Although bidders were given the opportunity to seek clarifications, key issues remained unclear. For example, although bidders had assumed that the license fee

would be treated as a current expenditure for purposes of computing taxable income, the Department of Revenue took the view that under Indian tax law it would have to be treated as a capital expenditure. It has subsequently been clarified that the license fee will be treated as a capital expenditure, with full amortization within the license period.

- Winning bidders ran into difficulties in reaching financial closure, because it was not clear whether the licenses could be assigned to lenders in the event of a debt service default. Lenders took the view that without assignability the projects could not be financed. It was subsequently agreed that these licenses could be assigned.

- Disputes arose over the interconnection charges levied on the new operators for connecting with the existing public sector system. The tender documents had not specified the interconnection charges, indicating only that they would be based on costs. Private operators claimed that the charges were much higher than justified, and the charges were subsequently reduced through consultation.

- The absence of a telecommunications regulatory authority meant that negotiations on points of dispute were conducted between new private operators and the Department of Telecommunications, which is also responsible for operating the public sector telephone system. This led to complaints from private sector operators of lack of transparency and fairness. A statutory regulatory authority has since been established.

---

for well-managed developing countries, foreign exchange risk management considerations may argue in favor of keeping the amount of foreign financing within reasonable limits.

There are limitations and constraints associated with each source of debt and equity financing, which should be kept in mind when devising financing packages for individual projects (table 6.1).

Equity financing

Private sector infrastructure projects require substantial equity financing, with higher equity requirements required for projects with higher levels of perceived risk. Project sponsors are an important source of equity, but they contribute only part of the total equity in most cases. Although preconstruction, or developmental,

costs represent only a small fraction of total cost in infrastructure projects, they can nevertheless run into several millions of dollars, all of which must be financed by equity provided by project sponsors.[6] Once the developmental phase ends, equity must be committed as part of the financing package. Sponsors typically commit a substantial proportion of total equity themselves, and they also tie up additional equity from other investors at this stage. Foreign sponsors may often be keen to link up with domestic investors at this stage on the grounds that this will reduce political risk. Domestic investors tend to evaluate risk less conservatively than foreign investors, and their involvement often helps to improve the perceptions of foreign investors.

Well-structured projects can expect to mobilize equity from international infrastructure funds specializing in investment in infrastructure projects. The Global Power Fund, which has a target of $1 billion, is an example of an infrastructure fund aimed at financing power projects in emerging markets. The AIG Asian Infrastructure Fund, which will invest $1 billion in the Asia-Pacific region, and the $750 million Asian Infrastructure Fund are examples of regional funds. The amounts available through these funds remain modest relative to the total requirement, but the pool of global capital they can tap is very large, and the flow of equity from this source could increase substantially if bankable projects become available and the track record of implementation improves. An important aspect of these funds is that they allow international investors to pool risks by investing in a mix of projects. They also enable institutional investors, who are relatively risk averse, to invest in infrastructure projects after the construction stage, when project risks are much lower. This provides valuable opportunities for "take-out" financing, enabling projects to be financed through the earlier and riskier stage by much larger involvement of equity from the sponsors or by high-cost debt, with a subsequent restructuring through attraction of equity from infrastructure funds through sale of sponsors' equity or refinancing of debt with equity.

A limited amount of equity support for private sector infrastructure is also available from multilateral organizations, such as the International Finance Corporation and the private sector window of the Asian Development Bank. Although these funds can provide only a small amount of capital, their participation in a project provides comfort to other investors.

The scope for raising equity from domestic capital markets is probably limited. Public utilities and domestic institutional investors may be willing to contribute part of the equity for project expansion, but significant domestic equity support may not be forthcoming for new infrastructure projects until there is a track record of performance. However, once project implementation proceeds and revenues begin to be generated through partial commissioning, it may be possible to tap a wider range of equity investors. This can be a useful financing strategy in the case of power projects with more than one generating unit or in telecommunications projects, in which the build up of line capacity occurs over time.

External debt financing

Several sources of external debt financing are available to well-structured private sector projects in countries with reasonable credit ratings.

Export credit agencies. Export credit agencies, which provide direct finance and guarantee commercial bank credit, have been the dominant source of international capital to finance infrastructure projects. In recent years export credit agencies have tended to guarantee bank loans. Traditionally, they funded public sector projects backed by sovereign guarantees, with some willingness in recent years to lend against guarantees of commercial banks. Unless the agencies can reorient themselves to provide financing without sovereign guarantees, their role in financing private sector infrastructure projects is likely to be limited.

International commercial banks. International commercial banks are the largest source of private finance for infrastructure development in developing countries. Of the $22.3 billion raised by developing countries for infrastructure financing in 1995, syndicated loans accounted for $13.5 billion, bonds for $5.3 billion, and equity for about $3.5 billion (World Bank 1997). Banks tend to be "hands-on" financiers, lending on the basis of a detailed analysis of project risk.

There are important limits to bank financing, however. The number of international banks actively involved in developing countries is small, and they are subject to exposure limits for projects and countries. This often leads to syndication, which involves cumbersome procedures. Another important limitation of commercial bank lending is the mismatch between the fifteen- to twenty-year loans needed by infrastructure projects and the seven- to ten-year maturities sought by international banks. Maturities of commercial bank loans can be lengthened from the beginning through multilateral guarantee support for later period repayments, as discussed later in this section. Reliance on bank financing

Table 6.1 Financing sources for private sector infrastructure

Domestic sources	External sources
Equity	
Domestic developers (independently or in collaboration with international developers)	International developers (independently or in collaboration with domestic developers)
Public utilities (taking minority holdings)	Equipment suppliers (in collaboration with domestic or international developers)
Other institutional investors (likely to be very limited)	Dedicated infrastructure funds
	Other international equity investors
	Multilateral agencies (International Finance Corporation, Asian Development Bank)
Debt	
Domestic commercial banks (3–5 years)	International commercial banks (7–10 years)
Domestic term lending institutions (7–10 years)	Export credit agencies (7–10 years)
Domestic bond markets (7–10 years)	International bond markets (10–30 years)
Specialized infrastructure financing institutions	Multilateral agencies (15–20 years)
	Bilateral aid agencies

for infrastructure projects must therefore be part of a mix involving other long-term lending, or it must be accompanied by suitable refinancing arrangements.

International bond markets. Bond financing is in many ways the ideal source of finance for infrastructure. Costs are higher than for syndicated loans, but maturities of ten to thirty years are typical, and even longer maturities are available for creditworthy issuers. Bond financing has been the fastest growing source of finance for developing countries in recent years, with total flows increasing from $2.3 billion in 1993 to $45.8 billion in 1996 (World Bank 1997). Its role remains modest, however, with only $5.3 billion provided in 1995 compared with $13.5 billion from syndicated loans.

One reason for the modest scale of bond financing of infrastructure is that access to international bond markets is not easy. Rule 144a and Regulation S of the U.S. Securities and Exchange Commission allow non-U.S. companies to raise capital in the United States from qualified institutional buyers without complying with the full listing procedures or conforming to generally accepted accounting practices. However, this window can be effectively tapped only by corporate bodies with relatively high credit ratings. Newly established infrastructure companies may find it difficult to access bond markets. Despite these limitations bond markets are likely to become increasingly important over time as more and more private sector infrastructure projects are successfully implemented in developing

countries, companies engaged in such projects gain financial recognition, and countries develop track records of successful implementation. Even new infrastructure companies may be able to access bond markets in the postconstruction stage, when risk perceptions have diminished and projects begin to generate steady revenue streams. Bond financing could be used in this way to refinance shorter-term loans taken initially to finance the construction stage.

The pricing of private corporate securities issued in international bond markets depends partly on corporate financial characteristics and partly on country characteristics. The efficiency of bond pricing can be enhanced by the existence of sovereign debt actively traded in the market. This increases country visibility, and therefore the appetite for corporate securities, and also provides a benchmark against which corporate debt can be efficiently priced. Issuing sovereign debt, however, implies that countries must be willing to accept continuous scrutiny of macroeconomic performance and economic policies by international credit rating agencies.

Multilateral institutions. Multilateral institutions, such as the World Bank and the Asian Development Bank, which have traditionally funded public sector infrastructure projects, are now willing to support private sector projects. The role of these agencies is necessarily limited, however. There are many competing claims on their scarce resources, and diversion of resources to fund private sector projects may represent no net gain for the economy. It can be argued, however, that these agencies can play an important catalytic role in the early stages of attracting the private sector into infrastructure. The transparency of their project evaluation procedures and their ability to benchmark an individual private sector project in a particular country against international experience of similar projects could help avoid controversies that may otherwise arise about private sector projects. Their active involvement as lenders in a project can also help reduce risk perception on the part of other investors. However, the procedures of these institutions are often too cumbersome to be acceptable to private sector investors.

The International Finance Corporation (IFC), the private sector arm of the World Bank Group, could play an important role in financing private sector infrastructure, but its scale of operations is relatively modest. The IFC's own commitments for infrastructure projects have increased from a little less than $200 million in 1990 to $727 million in 1996, and IFC syndication provided an additional $700 million in 1996. An important feature of IFC syndication in financing private sector infrastructure is that it has brought in nonbank financial institutions, including international insurance companies, to finance infrastructure projects in developing countries. A strong case can be made for much more extensive IFC involvement in financing private sector infrastructure projects in developing countries.

An innovative role played by multilateral institutions is the use of their guaranteeing capacity to extend the maturities of commercial loans to private sector infrastructure projects. The World Bank's partial credit guarantee is an example of such assistance. It was used to guarantee principal repayment from year eleven to year fifteen for a $150 million commercial bank loan for the Zhejiang project in China. Since China had access to commercial loans of only about six-year maturities at the time, the partial credit guarantee helped to extend even the uncovered period of commercial lending beyond the normal six-year period to ten years, after which the guarantee period extended it further to fifteen years. In the Philippines the partial credit guarantee has been used to support a $100 million ten-year bond issue by the National Power Corporation in the form of a put option

that enables the investors to present the bonds to the World Bank for principal repayment at maturity. The Asian Development Bank has also provided loan guarantees.

Bilateral aid agencies. Bilateral aid agencies have traditionally funded public sector infrastructure projects, but their role in funding private sector projects is likely to be very limited. Their resources are severely limited, and their priorities are shifting to social sector projects, making them reluctant to finance projects that are commercially financeable. However, like multilateral agencies, bilateral agencies could play an important catalytic role in the early stages of promoting private sector investment in infrastructure, especially by cofinancing private sector projects with multilateral agencies.

Domestic debt financing

Unlike the supply of external debt, which is plentiful, the supply of domestic debt is severely limited in most developing countries. Analysis of 140 private sector infrastructure projects from the IFC's portfolio shows that only a sixth of debt financing (which represented 61 percent of total project cost) was domestic debt (International Finance Corporation 1996). Moreover, all of the domestic debt was from local commercial banks, which do not provide long-term finance. This is clearly not a viable financing pattern. If private sector investment in infrastructure is to increase substantially, more domestic debt must be secured, and the composition of this debt must shift to longer maturities. This can happen only if domestic debt markets in developing countries develop.

Development of domestic debt markets

Domestic debt markets in developing countries are underdeveloped for many reasons, and action to develop these markets has to be taken on several fronts. A high rate of domestic savings is the most important structural prerequisite for ensuring an adequate flow of domestic finance for private infrastructure. High savings rates are not enough, however. Most East Asian economies, for example, have very high rates of savings, and yet debt markets in these economies are underdeveloped, with long-term debt particularly scarce.

A critical requirement for well-functioning debt markets is a sound macroeconomic balance, as reflected in modest fiscal deficits. High fiscal deficits have significant negative effects. If monetized they lead to inflation, which discourages savings in general and long-term saving in particular. If not monetized they put pressure on interest rates, which discourages investment, especially in projects with long gestation periods, such as infrastructure. High interest rates also tempt governments to intervene in financial markets to reduce the cost of government borrowing by forcing banks, insurance companies, provident funds, and pension funds to invest a high proportion of their assets in government securities. This reduces the cost of government borrowing, but it obviously does not eliminate the crowding out effect of high levels of government borrowing for nongovernment borrowers. In fact, the artificial lowering of interest rates on government securities distorts the government debt market, discouraging active trading in government securities and preventing the emergence of a reliable yield curve, all of which work against the development of an efficient debt market. Effective control over fiscal deficits is therefore an important element in any strategy for developing debt markets.

Another factor that helps to develop deep and liquid domestic debt markets is the existence of strong long-term contractual savings institutions, such as insurance companies and pension funds. These institutions have long-term liabilities and therefore have a natural interest in long-term debt instruments of high quality. Unfortunately, the insurance and pension funds sector is in an early stage of development in most developing countries. Statutory pre-emption of resources is high in many countries. In India insurance is also a public sector monopoly, although the government has recognized that reform of the insurance sector is linked to financing of infrastructure and has initiated a process of reform in this sector. An ideal environment for domestic debt markets is one in which domestic savings rates are high, fiscal deficits are low, and there is a strong insurance and pension fund segment in the financial sector.

Tax incentives for infrastructure financing. Faced with weak debt markets, many developing countries have sought to use tax incentives to stimulate a larger flow of domestic savings to infrastructure development. A wide variety of incentives are in use in many countries:

- The most popular incentive, available in China, India, and Thailand, is a tax holiday for the profits of private sector infrastructure projects. This instrument is not aimed specifically at domestic debt financing. However, it improves project profitability and thus enables the project to compete more effectively with other claimants for scarce domestic debt. The additional cash flow also enables the project to sustain larger debt service payments, thus enabling it to manage with shorter maturities, an important advantage where long-term debt is scarce.

- Incentives can also be directed at individual holders of equity or debt. In India, for example, long-term savings by individuals in the form of premiums for life insurance policies or contributions to the Provident Fund benefit from a tax credit. This incentive has been extended to investments in the shares or bonds of infrastructure projects. In a similar vein, capital gains on sale of shares have been exempted from taxation if the proceeds are invested in equity or debt instruments issued by infrastructure projects. These incentives do not distinguish between equity and debt, but they will help to attract debt financing into infrastructure.

- Tax incentives can also be aimed at financial intermediaries. Financial institutions in India are encouraged to provide long-term finance for infrastructure by allowing 40 percent of the profit attributable to such loans to be deducted from income in computing taxable income.

Tax incentives are criticized by purists on the grounds that they are indirect subsidies, which are usually not justifiable. But a good case can be made for such incentives, at least in the early stages of attracting private investment. The concern that tax incentives may lead to excessively high rates of return is fully met by ensuring a process of competition in fixing tariffs or license fees. Within such a framework tax incentives essentially allow private investors to provide services at lower cost to the consumer than would otherwise be possible. Since public sector suppliers benefit from various hidden subsidies (such as low-cost loans from the budget or provision of government equity on which a commercial rate of return is rarely earned or even planned for), the tax incentive serves only to level the playing field.

Innovative instruments with which to promote debt financing. Innovative financing instruments, such as the use of mezzanine debt, can sometimes attract domestic financing to infrastructure projects. Mezzanine debt refers to hybrid instruments that are somewhere between debt and equity (subordinated to secured debt but senior to equity in the hierarchy of creditors). A variety of such instruments, including simple subordinated debt, convertible debt, debt with stock warrants, and debt with an additional interest payment above the coupon rate contingent upon financial performance, exists. These instruments appeal to investors looking for higher returns than secured debt provides or for a share in the "up-side" risk of the project. Introduction of mezzanine debt in project financing for a given level of equity helps to improve the quality of senior debt and therefore its marketability.

There are several examples of the use of mezzanine debt in infrastructure financing in Asia. The Zhuhai Highway Company Ltd. raised $200 million in international capital markets, consisting of $85 million in senior notes and $115 million in subordinated notes. The Manila Skyway project relied on a combination of senior debt and mezzanine capital. The demand for mezzanine debt is also reflected in the emergence of dedicated mezzanine debt funds, such as the Asian Infrastructure Mezzanine Capital Fund, sponsored by the Prudential Capital Insurance Company. The ability to adopt a mixed strategy of relying on a combination of higher-cost mezzanine debt and lower-cost senior debt widens the pool of investors that can be tapped and can lower the overall financing cost of the project

The role of specialized financial institutions. Many countries have sought to address defi-

ciencies in their domestic debt markets by creating specialized institutions to deal with infrastructure financing. Examples of such institutions are the Pakistan Private Sector Energy Development Fund, established in 1988, which provides subordinated loans to private sector power projects, and the Jamaica Private Sector Energy Fund, established in 1992, which was set up to provide long-term finance. In India the Infrastructure Development Finance Company was recently set up as a private company, in which the government has a minority stake, with the objective of playing a catalytic role in channeling resources into commercially viable infrastructure projects (see box 6.3). A similar institution is being set up in Colombia.

Skepticism is sometimes expressed about whether creation of a specialized institution will improve financial intermediation. A new institution adds little if it only redirects resources that would have flowed from existing institutions to target sectors. Specialized institutions may appear to contribute additional resource flows if they are a conduit for government resources earmarked to support private sector infrastructure or if they are able to use government guarantees to obtain funds from the market at lower rates. However, the same subsidies could be extended just as effectively by channeling this support through existing financial institutions. It can be argued that because of their special mandate, specialized institutions will ensure a larger flow of funds to target sectors. If more financing flows to target sectors because these institutions are better able to find bankable infrastructure projects, then these institutions are providing valuable financial intermediation. If, however, more funds flow to target sectors because these institutions simply apply lower standards of credit appraisal in order to achieve some externally set target, the institutions may end up financing infrastructure projects that other financial institutions regard as unfinanceable on conventional criteria, and they will not be contributing to the efficiency of the financial markets.

The case for establishing a new institution therefore depends on whether it fills some critical gap in the financial environment facing infrastructure projects. Several such gaps justify creating a specialized financing institution:

- *Identification of financeable projects.* Specialized financing institutions may be able to identify financeable infrastructure projects more effectively and proactively than multipurpose financing institutions. Moreover, they may be able to help structure projects in a manner that makes them financeable, taking care to meet the complex risk mitigation requirements of different types of investors.
- *Take-out financing.* Infrastructure projects may need financing arrangements in which the project can be financed initially on the basis of shorter-term debt (such as credit from suppliers to finance equipment purchase) that is refinanced later by longer-term debt. A specialized institution could help guarantee such refinancing within a predetermined financing cost. This amounts to giving the project an assurance that if refinancing is not available on specified terms when needed, it will either be provided directly by the institution or the difference between the predetermined cost of financing and the cost at which funds can be raised will be reimbursed to the project. A commercial fee should, of course, be charged for this service.
- *Liquidity support.* Bond issuance by infrastructure projects can be encouraged by providing liquidity support for such bonds in the form of a put option prior to maturity or in the form of market making.
- *Securitization.* A specialized financing institution could securitize the cash flow from loans in a pool of successfully operating infrastructure projects, thus helping to create a wider market for such assets. Pooling of assets would help reduce risk through diversification and thus create a high-quality asset that could be effectively marketed to both domestic and international institutional investors.
- *Direct financing.* Conventional direct financing of infrastructure projects on a limited scale by a specialized institution may give confidence to other investors, which could leverage larger flows from other sources. This is especially true if the institution aims to fill critical financing gaps. The provision of subordinated loans, for example, helps to improve the quality of senior debt and may stimulate a larger flow of total resources at lower cost than would otherwise be possible.

A specialized institution can also play a very useful role as an interface between the government and new private investors in infrastructure. Many practical problems are likely to arise in the course of implementing private sector projects that may require constant review and modification of announced policies and also of the regulatory framework. A specialized financing institution with direct involvement in individual projects and with knowledge of domestic and international financial markets can help to identify problems and work cooperatively with government agencies to find solutions consistent with the requirements of financeability on the one hand and public concerns on the other.

The role of government guarantees

A general issue that arises in the context of financing private sector infrastructure projects is the role to be played by government guarantees. Private investors seek guarantees to cover a variety of circumstances. However, indiscriminate use of the government's guarantee power is not justifiable, since it involves a potential cost to the exchequer that becomes a real cost if the guarantee is invoked. Many projects that face financing problems are denied finance because of genuine deficiencies in financial viability. In such cases, the deficiencies must be remedied at the source rather than being covered by government guarantees.

In some situations, however, extension of government guarantees is necessary and appropriate. The most logical use of government guarantees is to cover events over which the government has full control, such as nationalization, government action that forces interruption of the project, or nonperformance of specific government obligations. In all these cases extension of government guarantees reduces the perception of risk and therefore costs. Government guarantees may also be sought to backstop obligations of government-controlled entities when the guarantees of these entities are not commercially acceptable. For example, private power producers selling power to public utilities may insist on guarantees from the government to cover nonpayment for power, or they may expect the government to backstop guarantees of public sector fuel suppliers against defaults in fuel supply agreements. In both cases government guarantees are insisted on because of the lack of financial credibility of the buying and supplying organizations directly involved. The ideal solution in such cases is to improve the financial viability of these organizations so that their own guarantees can be credible. This transformation is bound to take time, however. In fact, it may take several years after a credible restructuring process has been initiated before these organizations gain full financial credibility in financial markets. During this period the guarantees of these organizations may not be acceptable, and government guarantees may have to be provided as an interim arrangement. Extension of government guarantees in these circumstances can be justified, provided the projects meet high standards of viability and the more fundamental corrective steps are under way. In order to minimize the extent of guarantee exposure, the guarantees can be structured to include "fall-away" provisions, which are triggered as soon as certain credit benchmarks are achieved (Johnston, Mody, and Shanks 1996).

Conclusion

Despite active pursuit of private investment in infrastructure by most developing countries and a growing number of success stories, the pace of such investment remains slower than initially expected. The main reason is that the preconditions for private financing of infrastructure are more difficult to establish than is commonly realized. Inadequate preparatory work leads to unanticipated problems and delays in implementing private sector infrastructure projects.

One set of problems arises because infrastructure sectors are invariably subject to tariff regulation, and it is difficult to strike a balance between ensuring that tariffs are sufficiently remunerative to private investors and ensuring that they are seen as fair to consumers. Consumer acceptance is especially a problem where consumers have grown accustomed to unrealistically low tariffs charged by public sector systems, reflecting large explicit or implicit subsidies. Since similar subsidies cannot be extended to the private sector—indeed, their continuation even for the public sector may not be feasible—a shift to more viable tariffs is unavoidable. Unless the need for this shift is widely accepted, it will be difficult to attract private investment in infrastructure.

Even where the need for higher tariffs is accepted in principle, tariffs charged by private sector suppliers may still attract criticism if they are perceived as too high. Economic efficiency requires that private sector projects should represent least-cost options. This objective is difficult to realize. Cost-based formulas for determining tariffs make it difficult to ensure that efficiency considerations have been fully observed: the padding of costs is difficult to detect and leads to unduly high tariffs and inflated rates of return. Competitive bidding is the only transparent method of resolving this problem. It must be recognized, however, that the effectiveness of competitive bidding depends critically on the quality of the bidding process.

Risks associated with infrastructure projects also pose special problems in implementation. Many of the risks are common to any commercial venture and can be handled in proven ways. But other risks are unique to infrastructure, for example, those arising from interface with regulatory authorities and with other government-dominated agencies. These risks can be reduced to acceptable levels through explicit risk sharing arrangements that define the compliance obligations of the government and government agencies and specify penalties for default. But these arrangements are complex and are very different from the normal ones with public sector suppliers. Governments are sometimes reluctant to enter into these arrangements and often do not appreciate the need for them from the investor's point of view.

Independent regulatory authorities with a clear mandate to ensure fair treatment for private sector suppliers help to reduce perceptions of risk, as does an efficient legal system that provides quick redress, especially in matters relating to contract enforcement. Few countries have all these institutions in place, however, and deficiencies in this area explain some of the delay in project implementation.

Financial markets also impose constraints on project implementation. Once remunerative tariff structures and acceptable risk mitigation arrangements are in place, projects have to achieve financial closure. This requires mobilizing an appropriate mix of financing in terms of equity and debt. Infrastructure projects require long debt maturities, reflecting the long payback period. In the absence of long-term debt, they need reasonable assurance of refinancing or take-out financing.

Availability of domestic finance is perhaps the most serious constraint on infrastructure financing. Infrastructure projects cannot be financed exclusively or even primarily through external capital, if only because tariffs are usually fixed in domestic currency and a large share of foreign currency financing implies a correspondingly high foreign exchange risk. A substantial share of project costs must therefore be domestically financed. Domestic debt financing is likely to pose a special problem because most developing countries do not have well-developed domestic debt markets and long-term debt is especially scarce. Measures to develop domestic debt markets are therefore crucial to support private sector infrastructure projects.

By contrast, external capital is more plentiful for well-structured projects in countries perceived as investor-friendly and creditworthy—both restrictive criteria, but applicable to a large number of countries. The pool of international debt and equity capital available for such projects is fairly large and could grow substantially as private sector projects are seen to operate successfully in more and more countries. As with domestic finance, the biggest problem is accessing long-term debt. International bond markets are the logical source for such capital, but access to these markets remains limited, especially for new companies implementing projects on a non-recourse basis. Credit enhancement through partial credit risk guarantees of the type now being offered by multilateral development banks may be helpful in improving access to bond markets.

The development of domestic debt markets requires an environment of fiscal prudence with moderate fiscal deficits that do not put pressure on domestic interest rates. It also requires the development of an efficient and liquid market for government debt, which provides the foundation for developing a broader market for corporate debt. And it requires the development of institutions engaged in mobilizing long-term savings, especially insurance and pension funds, which have a natural appetite for high-quality, long-term debt.

No country presents an ideal combination of circumstances, and experience shows that there are many ways of solving problems that constrain such investment—ways that differ from project to project and country to country. Financial markets show great scope for innovation in tailoring financing solutions to financing needs. Policies need to be flexible to allow such innovation to flourish.

The problems discussed here appear formidable, and indeed they are. But despite these problems an increasing number of private sector projects are being implemented in an ever-growing number of countries. Greater clarity in policy and proactive efforts by governments to create the conditions necessary to attract private investment in infrastructure will result in successful implementation of more and more projects. This favorable experience will improve expectations among investors and reduce perceptions of risk. That should help to accelerate a process that is clearly already under way, though still lacking the momentum that is needed and that is also feasible.

Notes

Montek S. Ahluwalia is finance secretary of India. The views expressed in this paper are his own and do not necessarily reflect the views of the government of India. Acknowledgments are due to Gajendra Haldea, Harinder Kohli, Edwin Lim, Ashoka Mody, and Teh Kok Peng for helpful comments on an earlier version of this chapter.

1. In periods of high inflation even the periodicity of the adjustment can become an important factor, since too long a delay may cause significant erosion in profitability.

2. New licensees are typically either given monopoly access to the market or face only limited competition. In India, for example, the market has been divided into thirteen subdivisions (circles) for telecommunications licensing. Bids have been solicited for one additional supplier of basic (fixed telephone) services in each circle to compete with the existing public sector service. Cellular telephones are entirely in the private sector, and bids have been solicited for two competing suppliers per circle.

3. In principle it is possible for fully priced private sector supply of services to be cheaper than underpriced public sector services because of greater operational efficiency. This effect may not offset the effect of hidden subsidies in all cases, however.

4. The Don Muang Tollway in Thailand has suffered from inadequate traffic because the government did not dismantle the untolled flyovers, which were to have been torn down as part of the concession agreement. Consumer preference for continuing with the toll-free option proved stronger than expected, because the charging segment was not perceived as generating benefits commensurate with costs.

5. The view that shifting risks from one part of the public sector to another serves no purpose is erroneous. Even within a public sector framework, clear assignment of risk to individual public sector entities, with incentives for risk management, would increase the effort made by individual entities to avoid the contingency involved. For example, a fuel supply agreement between a public sector supplier of fuel and a public sector producer of power with penalties for nonperformance is likely to create incentives for the fuel supplier that will reduce disruptions in fuel supply.

6. Risk is also highest at this stage, since there is no certainty that a satisfactorily negotiated project will emerge. Project sponsors typically expect to reap very high returns on this portion of the investment. The high return to sponsors for preconstruction investment can be manifested in purchase of part of the sponsors' equity at a substantial premium by new investors brought in at the time of financial closure. The same result is achieved by charging a premium for fresh equity by new investors brought in at the stage of project implementation.

References

International Finance Corporation. 1996. *Financing Private Infrastructure*. Lessons of Experience Series 4. Washington, D.C.

Johnston, Felton Mac, Ashoka Mody, and Robert Shanks. 1996. "A House of Cards." *Project and Trade Finance* (February): 40–42.

World Bank. 1997. *Global Development Finance*, Vol. 1. Washington, D.C.